A Plague of Hunger

A Plague of Hunger

by Gene Erb

Photographs by Bob Modersohn
Warren Taylor
Gene Erb

Iowa State University Press / Ames

129832

Gene Erb, a graduate of Iowa State University with a masters degree from the University of Missouri, lives in West Des Moines, Iowa, and writes about business, labor, agriculture, and the economy for *The Des Moines Register.*

Robert J. Modersohn III, a graduate of Drake University and resident of Des Moines, Iowa, is a *Des Moines Register* staff photographer specializing in rural and agricultural subjects.

Warren Taylor, a graduate of Drake University, lives in Des Moines and is director of photography for *The Des Moines Register.*

The material included in *A Plague of Hunger,* text and photographs, appeared originally in *The Des Moines Register* and is reprinted with permission. The publisher and the author wish to thank the *Register* for its cooperation throughout the publication process.

© 1990 Iowa State University Press, Ames, Iowa 50010

Manufactured in the United States of America
♾ This book is printed on acid-free paper.

First edition, 1990

Library of Congress Cataloging-in-Publication Data

Erb, Gene.
   A plague of hunger / by Gene Erb : photographs by Bob Modersohn, Warren Taylor, Gene Erb.
      p.   cm.
   ISBN 0-8138-0962-2
   1. Food supply—Developing countries. 2. Poor—Developing countries. 3. Agriculture—Economic aspects—Developing countries. 4. Food relief—Developing countries. I. Title.
HD9018.D44E72   1990   90-32423
363.8′09172′4—dc20

For my family, friends, and colleagues who supported me;
for the dedicated people who assisted me;
and most importantly, for the children, women, and men
who struggle every day to survive.

CONTENTS

FOREWORD

FEW ASTUTE OBSERVERS of the contemporary scene would quibble with the assertion that, next to arms control, hunger is the most important problem facing the human family. Whether viewed starkly in terms of human suffering or in terms of the potential for social and political unrest, malnutrition and starvation persist as unwelcome legacies of the ages. With all of our technological and scientific cleverness, we have been unable to overcome all of the economic, institutional and political barriers to solving the hunger dilemma.

In this volume, Gene Erb has painted an unusually perceptive portrait of the hunger situation. Writing in a manner and style that capture the human dimensions of the tragedy on the one hand and the causative factors on the other, Erb has presented an eloquent case for urgency in cutting through the political and economic obstacles to resolution of the hunger problem.

As can be seen clearly from Erb's series of in-depth articles, the problem is indeed complex. Fundamentally, it is a problem of poverty, low income, and low personal productivity. Countries with significant levels of malnutrition and starvation simply do not produce enough of what the rest of the world wants and is willing to pay for in trade. Food is available in abundance but just out of reach for low-income consumers around the world. This is one of the cruelest paradoxes of modern times—hunger in the midst of plenty. At present price relationships, agriculture in many areas of the developed world has been experiencing overproduction and surpluses while parts of Latin America, Asia, and Africa have experienced starvation.

As Erb observes, the problem is more than economic. Outmoded institutions have blocked growth and development. Undemocratic political systems have siphoned off gains that should have gone to improve levels of nutrition. Unwise restraints on price relationships have discouraged food production and perpetuated capital scarcity in the agricultural sectors of too many Third World countries.

But above all the culprit is low income. The last frontier for increasing the demand for food is the Third World. Until incomes rise, however, that potential demand will not become effective demand. Incomes won't rise without economic development—education, health care, highways, harbors, the entire infrastructure. Thus, economic assistance will be needed, with a payoff measured in decades, not in years.

Erb points out, poignantly, compelling reasons why the United States and other developed nations should be about that task. His is a compelling story; I commend it to you as a moving essay on an important feature of the human condition in the latter part of the twentieth century.

Ames, Iowa

NEIL E. HARL

INTRODUCTION

MY FIRST STEP into the Third World as a journalist was taken on a bright day in February 1986, at the border between southern California and northern Baja—a well-fortified line separating affluence from poverty. Behind me sprawled the American dream—San Diego's freeways flowing with cars and motor homes, glittering discos and high-rise hotels, chic shops, ornate office parks, majestic mansions, and lush lawns reaching into the hills. Before me sprawled Mexican reality—Tijuana's pitted roads filled with belching buses and battered cars, beggars seeking handouts, children hustling shoe shines, women selling trinkets, squalid tenements, cardboard shantytowns, and humble homes perched tenuously on barren hills.

For the next two weeks I traveled the Mexican side of the border from the Pacific Ocean to the Gulf of Mexico, investigating the explosive growth of U.S.-owned plants called "maquiladoras," where workers "move perilously between destitution and mere subsistence, even while surrounded by the glitter of 'progress,'" according to Maria Patricia Fernandez-Kelly, a maquiladora expert at the University of California at San Diego. Everywhere I stopped, I found hard-working Mexicans struggling to survive and American executives who accepted their struggles as an economic fact of life.

Photographer Warren Taylor [left] *and reporter Gene Erb on assignment in Mexico in 1986.*

☐ There was Sanjuana, a Tijuana woman working eight hours a day, six days a week for a daily pay of just $4. The income from her job making toys for a Mexican subsidiary of Iowa's Ertl Co. was not enough to feed her children a balanced, healthy diet, let alone enough to buy them any of the toys she made. Sanjuana lived in the steep, unstable hills on the outskirts of town in a humble dwelling with no heat, sewer, or tap water. Her long days began at 5:00 A.M. and ended late in the evening. Still, she could afford to feed herself and her four children little more than tortillas and atole, a hot drink made of flour, powdered milk, and water. The operations manager at Sanjuana's plant said he "felt a little sorry for the people" when he first started working at the Ertl plant. "But you do get a little callous. You can't help it."

☐ There was the vice president with A. C. Nielsen Company's coupon-sorting subsidiary, who said Nielsen moved coupon-sorting jobs from Iowa to Ciudad Juarez "to take advantage of the lower costs of doing business. You have to go where you can get the least expensive fingers and toes to sort the coupons, and we have some very good ones. We can be very selective. There are plenty of people to choose from." The executive said Nielsen had to seek out people willing to work for subsistence wages: "We've got to keep costs down to keep the program attractive to manufacturers. They will stop using coupons if the costs of handling run too high . . . so it's more of a survival thing than a competitive thing."

☐ There was the general manager of Iowa-based Winegard Company's subsidiary in Matamoros, who said the electronics firm opened the Mexican plant because it was "getting clobbered by Far East companies. What we're really down here for is to take care of the labor-intensive things." The Third World beckoned, he said: "Haiti's got a tremendous program. Their wages can compete with anybody's wages in the world. You give them a chicken head and a bowl of soup and they're happy."

Tortillas, chicken heads and atole made with unsafe water – a recipe for disease, hunger, suffering, and death.

I hadn't expected to get the chance to explore this recipe further, even though I knew I had just scratched the surface of the hunger topic in my maquiladora series. In December 1987, however, Iowa State University economics professor Neil Harl and I had a thought-provoking discussion about the political and economic causes of world hunger and about plans for a World Food Conference entitled "Hunger in the Midst of Plenty" to be held in June 1988 in Des Moines. "I view hunger as the most important single problem, next to arms control, facing the world today," Harl said.

The more I thought about it, the more convinced I became that world hunger would be a natural subject of investigation for the *The Des Moines Register,* a newspaper keenly interested in food and agriculture issues located in the center of one of the world's richest food-producing regions. I made a formal proposal to the *Register's* editors, suggesting that we visit two or three countries with chronic hunger problems and at least one Third World country where significant progress has been made against poverty and hunger. I noted that at two previous World Food Conferences, one in Rome in 1974 and one in Ames in 1976, the focus had been on the need to increase agricultural production to feed a burgeoning world population.

"The food has been produced—enough to provide every man, woman and child on earth 3,600 calories a day—yet one-fifth of the world's population is chronically hungry," I noted in my proposal. ". . . It is a complex, controversial subject, one which I believe the *Register*

Honduras: Paula Corrales makes tortillas for her seven children in a cornstalk lean-to next to her one-room shack.

ought to explore. Ideally a series on the subject would run the week before the June 5 World Food Conference. It certainly would give those attending some new food for thought."

The response was immediate and enthusiastic. Editor James Gannon said he didn't know how the *Register* could afford to tackle the project, especially in a tight-budget election year, but he didn't know how the paper could afford not to do it, either. I immediately began research and travel plans for the series. After exhaustive research and consultation with hunger experts, I proposed travel to five countries where I could explore different aspects of the hunger dilemma:

HONDURAS, the poorest nation in the Western Hemisphere after Haiti with the highest infant mortality rate in Central America. Its poverty and hunger problems in 1988 were tied to land and wealth distribution and were typical of the severe problems in Latin America. Most of the land was owned or controlled by a small wealthy class or by foreign corporations like United Brands Company, producer of Chiquita Brands bananas, and Castle & Cooke Incorporated, producer of Dole bananas and pineapples. Peasants there, like peasants in many Latin American nations, had been forced off land where they used to grow food. Some were trying to farm marginal land on steep hillsides. Some lived in squalor and begged in overcrowded cities. Some worked for sub-subsistence wages in plants and on plantations. The Nicaraguan war, interests of large corporations, internal corruption, and a lender-encouraged shift from subsistence farming to export cattle ranching had all played a part in the hunger and death of poor Hondurans.

ETHIOPIA, the world's symbol of hunger in the 1980s and a case study in how national and world leaders can cause incomprehensible human suffering. Famine claimed 1 million lives in Ethiopia in 1984–85. The famine was triggered by drought, but a long history of oppression and exploitation of the Ethiopian people set the stage for the tragedy. Emperor Haile Selassie's feudal monarchy was overthrown in 1974, only to be replaced by an oppressive Marxist military dictatorship that has had to fight numerous rebellions. Internal strife was causing much of the suffering, but government policies also had taken their toll. Agricultural development had gone to state farms while peasant farmers, forced to sell their crops to the government at low prices, had little reason to produce more than they needed for subsistence. Food shortages had become so severe by the late 1980s that the threat of famine had become a chronic condition, according to the United Nations. Nev-

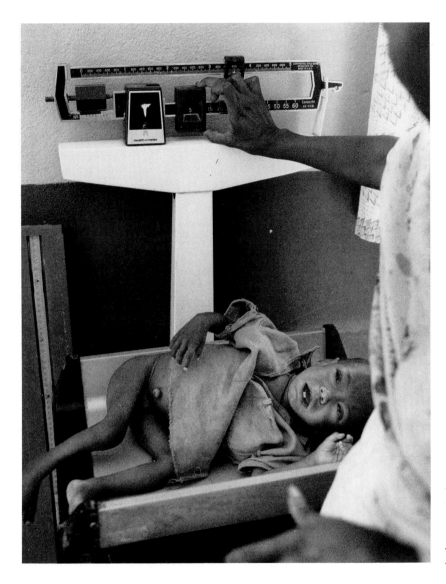

Ethiopia: At Tigre's Latchi clinic, malnourished 2-year-old Gabryzehare Halafome weighs in at just 10½ pounds.

ertheless, U.N. studies have found that the nation could produce enough food to feed a population two to three times Ethiopia's size with proper development.

EGYPT, land of the enigmatic sphinx, was receiving half of all U.S. food aid to Africa in the 1980s, not because it was the country with the greatest need but because of its strategic importance in both northern

Egypt: Samira and her daughter sift through trash for food in the garbage village they call home in Cairo.

Africa and the Middle East. The country's $189.2 million in U.S. food aid in 1987 was 36 times the amount allocated to famine-plagued Ethiopia. Yet, even with food, economic and development assistance totaling about $1 billion a year, Egypt's poorest people remained chronically hungry. The U.S. food program in Egypt was rife with corruption and inefficiencies. Of some $220 million in 1986 food aid, only $6.6 million went directly to those in need. The rest was given to the Egyptian government, which sold it to mills, bakeries, and other food businesses for distribution at subsidized prices to all Egyptians, from the poorest to the wealthiest. Thousands of Cairo's poor, meanwhile, lived in villages built in garbage dumps, where they sorted through refuse for food to eat and scraps to sell.

ZIMBABWE, an infant southern African nation, gained independence and black majority rule in April 1980 after more than 100 years of

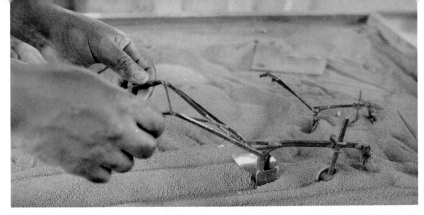

Zimbabwe: Scale model plow helps teach tillage techniques.

rule by the white minority. The new government, following a policy of more equitable distribution of wealth, food, land, education, and health services, had made remarkable progress in reducing hunger. Black peasant farmers, provided price incentives, technical support, financing, and marketing channels, had more than tripled their corn production. The small farmers' share of marketed produce had risen from 10 percent in 1980 to 38 percent in 1985, and the value of the corn and cotton sales had grown from $17 million to $218 million. The infant mortality rate had been cut to 60 per 1,000 infants in 1987 from 110 per 1,000 in 1960, and the new government had worked to see that everyone had an adequate diet, even in times of drought. Still, Zimbabwe was suffering from South Africa–sponsored economic destabilization and guerrilla ac-

Zimbabwe: Philemon Gwangwava gets his real plow ready.

tivity. The government was spending about $2 million a day defending its southern and eastern borders and a vital rail line from Zimbabwe through Mozambique to the Indian Ocean.

SOUTH KOREA is one of the countries U.S. Agency for International Development officials point to as a food and development success story. United States aid there has helped transform The Republic of Korea from a hunger-plagued, underdeveloped country into an emerging economic power that has conquered its hunger problems. South Korea instituted important land distribution and agrarian reforms in the 1950s and 1960s. New high-yielding rice varieties produced a "green revolution" in the 1970s that made the nation self-sufficient in its basic food staple. At the same time, farmers thrived because of rural economic development, technical assistance, financing for inputs, and crop price supports.

The stories about these countries and others, contained in Part I, cover a broad spectrum of hunger-related situations and issues. Some updating and expansion is appropriate, however, particularly in the areas of regional conflict and economic destabilization, looming population problems, and the roles agrarian reform and economic development could play in resolving these problems.

At the time of this writing in 1989, regional conflicts and economic destabilization were causing or exacerbating chronic hunger and famine in many areas of Africa, Latin America, and Asia.

Tens of thousands of people were dying of hunger in southern Sudan, and hundreds of thousands more were expected to die—not because of a lack of food to feed them but because food had become a weapon. Most of the victims were Dinka tribe members caught in a civil war between the northern-based Islamic government and the Southern Peoples Liberation Army, a Christian and animist group that recruits from the Dinkas. The Sudanese government, supported with U.S. food and development aid, was impeding food shipments to southern areas where the Dinkas live, and was arming the Dinkas' enemies with modern weapons. Some feared the government was bent on exterminating the Dinkas. In neighboring Ethiopia, both rebels and government troops were exacerbating hunger. Rebels backed by Arab nations had mined supply roads and attacked emergency food convoys, and the Soviet-backed government had slowed relief efforts in rebel-held areas.

In southern Africa, the South African government had been waging

South Korea: A supermarket employee in Seoul carries a tray of beef roasts. Consumption of meat and dairy products is increasing rapidly in Korea.

economic and military war against its own black citizens and against the peoples of nine neighboring black-governed countries for years, aggravating chronic hunger problems and creating famine conditions in Mozambique and Angola. "The impact of drought on Africa has been vividly brought home in literally thousands of news reports and television programmes. But in southern Africa, the impact of war and apartheid has often been greater than that of drought . . . ," says a report prepared for UNICEF. Since independence in 1975, hardly a week had passed in peace in more than 13 years in Mozambique and Angola.

Rural clinics and schools had been destroyed and agricultural production disrupted. Rural residents had abandoned good farming areas to escape rape, mutilation and death at the hands of South Africa–backed rebels. "One of the deadliest weapons" in southern Africa has been "mass terrorism carried out by forces which have burned crops and farmhouses, pillaged and destroyed schools, clinics, churches, mosques, stores and villages. . . . In Angola and Mozambique, teachers, nurses, agricultural technicians, engineers and geologists have been killed and kidnapped, maimed and mutilated," the United Nations Children's Fund (UNICEF) report says. "The carnage has been indiscriminate, with infants and children not exempted."

At the same time, the world's superpowers – the United States, the Soviet Union and China – were contributing to hunger by destabilizing economies or backing either rebels or government troops in Angola, Ethiopia, Afghanistan, Cambodia, Nicaragua, Guatemala, El Salvador, and many other countries around the world. "The way people perceive war here is that it is the giants fighting in Africa," a University of Zimbabwe professor told me during my research there. "They have to fight some way, and so they're doing it through the people of Africa."

An increase in U.S. military aid to Honduras, Guatemala, and El Salvador in the 1980s was accompanied by an escalation of government human rights violations, kidnappings, torture, and murder. Thousands of peasants, mostly Indians, had been displaced, persecuted, terrorized or murdered by government troops and death squads in Guatemala, and unexplained murders and disappearances had increased in Honduras. A November 1987 report by Iowa Congressman Jim Leach and two other members of the Arms Control and Foreign Policy Caucus found that $608 million in U.S. aid to El Salvador – three-quarters of which went to the military – was "perpetuating" the five-year civil war there. The report noted a ten-fold rise in unemployment since the war began, a drop in real wages, and a rise in the poverty rate. Half the population was under- or unemployed in 1987, one in ten Salvadorans lived in refugee camps, the infant mortality rate had jumped 36 percent and one of every four children was malnourished. The Leach report concluded, "In the absence of a major shift in the focus of U.S. policy toward El Salvador and the nature of U.S. assistance to that country, economic and social conditions [will] continue to deteriorate."

There were some halting steps toward the resolution of conflicts in 1988 and 1989. The Soviet Union had agreed to withdraw its troops from Afghanistan – the country with the world's highest rate of hunger-related deaths – and the United States had agreed to stop supporting rebels in the civil war there. Also, efforts were under way to resolve conflicts in Central America, Angola, Sudan, Ethiopia, Cambodia, Iran, and Iraq. The potential for continued conflict remained in all of these areas, however.

The world's population did not reach 1 billion until somewhere around 1800. It hit the 2 billion mark just 30 years later, 3 billion in 1960, 4 billion in 1974 and 5 billion in 1985. Demographers expected the world's population to top 6 billion by the year 2000, and they expected most of the growth would occur in Third World countries, where burgeoning populations threatened to undermine the fight against hunger by outpacing economic growth and the growth in food production. Africa's population, at 481 million in 1980, was expected to hit 872 million by the year 2000. Asia's was expected to increase from 2.55 billion to 3.55 billion during the same period; Central America's from 92 million to 149 million; and South America's from 240 million to 356 million.

These predictions were expected to come true even if developing nations managed to implement effective family planning programs. Third World nations in the 1980s were faced with tremendous baby booms that had created youthful populations—booms that would make it impossible to stem their population tides for decades to come, even with effective education and social and economic incentives to limit family size. More than half of the 47 million people in Ethiopia, for instance, were under 20 years of age in 1988. Even dramatic declines in fertility would not prevent the continuing growth of the number of adults reaching childbearing age there for two or three decades. Other countries faced similar problems. With effective family planning programs, however, demographers predicted these large groups of young people would pass through the childbearing years and nations would have the opportunity to get a grasp on population growth. Progress would not come, however, without significant improvement in the economic status of poor people. Large families—children to generate income—provide the only economic security many poor people have, especially in old age. Demographers generally agree they will not cut family size until they are economically secure.

Many economists believe poverty, social unrest, conflict and hunger will continue to grow in the twenty-first century unless steps are taken to encourage agrarian reform and agricultural development in poor countries. Land distribution, price supports, and improvements in marketing, credit, and agricultural extension have sparked dramatic economic improvements in Taiwan and South Korea and were working wonders in Zimbabwe in the late 1980s. Reforms in these countries have helped distribute wealth and improve the economic status of large rural populations. Success is not automatic, however. Land reform without other reforms and rural development have been largely unsuccessful in many countries. Governments in Latin America have passed land reform laws only in response to threats of political or social instability. A commitment to make the laws work and to support peasant farmers with progressive agricultural policies has been conspicuously absent. Control of most land has remained in the hands of foreign interests and wealthy individuals, and massive poverty and hunger have persisted. Peasants who have taken title to land under the reform law in Honduras have not enjoyed the support small farmers have received in Zimbabwe. Indeed, they have had to contend with hostilities from the ruling elite. More than 1,000 Brazilian peasants trying to hold their land or to claim rights to land under a reform law there have been brutally killed by thugs hired by wealthy landowners. Reforms also have failed in countries like Marxist Ethiopia and socialist Egypt, where agricultural and economic policies have eliminated incentives to produce and have served those in power instead of the poor and hungry.

Complex issues — agrarian reform, agricultural development, U.S. aid, Third World debt, population growth, and regional conflict — swirl around the question of hunger. There is nothing complex about the root cause, however. Hunger in the midst of plenty is caused by greed — the sort of greed that leads corporations to pay people less than they need to eat, that leads to genocide by power-hungry fanatics and ideologues in Sudan and Ethiopia, that keeps land and wealth concentrated in the hands of a few, that reduces and misdirects U.S. food and economic aid, that drains Third World countries of their meager natural and financial resources. The newspaper stories in this book address all of these issues, including greed, which is described eloquently by an African woman in the book's epilogue. The Mexico stories were published in *The Des Moines Register* in March 1986 and the hunger stories were published in late May and early June of 1988. The stories are dated in the sense that they are about specific people, situations, and conditions at a point in time. Hunger, however, has dogged mankind from the beginning of time. Some of the problems addressed in this book have been with us for decades, others for thousands of years. Many are likely to be with us for years, perhaps decades, to come. One would hope, however, that "A Plague of Hunger" would soon become truly dated, a chronicle of an earlier, harsher time when hunger plagued the world.

I. Starvation amid Plenty

1. A World of Hunger

CAIRO, EGYPT—Samira and her teen-age daughter, Fayza, sit in filth and stench, sorting through garbage in search of food to eat and scraps to sell. They are among the nearly 100,000 poor and hungry "garbage people" who are forced to live off trash collected from the streets of Cairo.

"Can you imagine, going through garbage, sorting it, and then eating it?" asks Lila Camel, an Egyptian volunteer who works with the garbage people.

In Honduras, hospitals overflow with malnourished, listless children, unable to muster a smile or chew solid food. One skeleton-thin boy, Maises Banegas Anarriba, lies in a bed with brittle broken bones, barely breathing. He is too weak to move or make a sound. His mother insists she has fed him well—tortillas, milk, beans—every day. But she is lying, too ashamed to admit she can't care for her son.

In northern Ethiopia, Megesete Desta pleads for a greater portion of emergency food because she is hungry and her breasts are too dry to feed her son. Father Gianni Premoli must tell her angrily that there is no extra food; there is not even enough to feed all the starving people.

From Latin America to Africa and Asia, a plague of hunger encircles the globe. And yet, the world overflows with food. It is a paradox that has perplexed some of the most sophisticated thinkers of the 20th century.

Consider: Enough grain alone is produced each year to feed every man, woman and child on Earth a plentiful 3,600 calories a day. More-

Register *photographer Robert Modersohn on assignment in Cairo, Egypt.*

*Gene Erb with Ethio-
pian boys at an emer-
gency feeding center
in Mekele, Ethiopia.*

over, there is enough high-quality farmland in the world to produce even more food than that. But for several complex reasons, the world has not found a way to deliver all that food to the people who need it most. Nor is all that land used to benefit the hungry. What's wrong? There are as many answers to that question as there are hungry countries. Here is a sampling.

—In Honduras, the best farmland is controlled by the wealthy and by large U.S. companies. Your last double cheeseburger may have been made with Honduran beef, your last bunch of bananas picked from a Honduran plantation. Moreover, the United States government has helped underwrite an expansion of the country's cattle industry, which has driven peasant farmers off the land and left Honduras the poorest, hungriest country in Central America.

—In Ethiopia, internal war, national government policies and the policies of the Soviet Union and the United States have combined to starve its people. The Marxist government refuses to negotiate with powerful Marxist rebels. The Soviets prolong the stalemate with government military assistance. And the United States sits on the sidelines, until many Ethiopians are near death, before offering food because it doesn't want to support a communist regime.

—In Egypt, U.S. generosity abounds. Food and money pour in to the tune of $1 billion a year—with few strings attached. U.S. wheat is used to subsidize bread prices for all, the cash is used to keep a bloated government afloat, while continued inefficiencies and misguided policies leave millions of Egyptians on the edge of starvation. These and other problems are keeping a fifth of the world's population chronically hungry.

Grim reminders of hunger are everywhere in Third World countries:

In heaps of dirt where jagged rocks and rusted bowls mark graves of famine victims.
In the anguished faces of mothers.
In wails of half-starved babies at clinics and infant feeding tents.

"Almost without notice, more than 14 million children are now dying every year," says the United Nations International Children's

Emergency Fund. "They are dying in the final coma of dehydration . . . dying in the long-drawn-out process of frequent 'ordinary' illnesses, which steadily weaken and malnourish the body until it has nothing left to fight the next cold, or the next fever, or the next bout of diarrhea.

". . . It makes no moral difference that these millions of children did not die in any one particular place at any one particular time. But it does mean that their suffering cannot be framed in the viewfinder of a camera. And it does mean that their deaths are therefore not news, and that the world is not shamed into action on their behalf."

The Byzantine politics of world food production – driven by everything from civil wars to drought to U.S. foreign policy – have kept dozens of countries from being able to feed their own people.

The price of hunger is suffering and death, disruption of national economies, depression of world agricultural markets, and a threat to global security.

"I view hunger as the most important single problem, next to arms control, facing the world today," said Neil Harl, an Iowa State University economist and organizer of a world food conference held in Des Moines the week of June 6, 1988.

There have been two previous world food conferences – one in Rome, Italy, in 1974 and another in Ames, Iowa, in 1976. At each, the mandate was increasing food production. But despite impressive gains in food production, more people go hungry today than ever before. More than 1 billion people are chronically hungry, 700 million so weakened that they suffer from stunted growth and severe health risks, according to a World Bank report on poverty and hunger.

The United Nations says this "silent emergency" of chronic hunger takes more lives than famine, more lives each year than were lost in all of World War II – an estimated 18 million to 20 million annually, 35,000 each day, 24 every minute.

The U.N. defines hunger as a chronic, societywide condition in which a country's infant mortality rate is greater than 50 deaths per 1,000 infants. Using that standard, UNICEF says hunger is a chronic problem in 71 nations.

The infant mortality rates are much higher in many of those countries. Afghanistan, Mali, Sierra Leone, Malawi, Guinea, Ethiopia, and Somalia, for example, all have mortality rates above 150 per 1,000 infants. That compares with 11 deaths per 1,000 infants in the United States and six per 1,000 in Finland and Sweden.

Yet the world is awash in surplus food. Food production over the

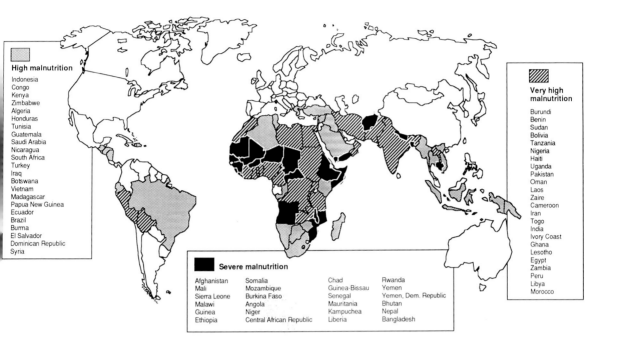

High malnutrition

Indonesia
Congo
Kenya
Zimbabwe
Algeria
Honduras
Tunisia
Guatemala
Saudi Arabia
Nicaragua
South Africa
Turkey
Iraq
Botswana
Vietnam
Madagascar
Papua New Guinea
Ecuador
Brazil
Burma
El Salvador
Dominican Republic
Syria

Very high malnutrition

Burundi
Benin
Sudan
Bolivia
Tanzania
Nigeria
Haiti
Uganda
Pakistan
Oman
Laos
Zaire
Cameroon
Iran
Togo
India
Ivory Coast
Ghana
Lesotho
Egypt
Zambia
Peru
Libya
Morocco

Severe malnutrition

Afghanistan	Somalia	Chad	Rwanda
Mali	Mozambique	Guinea-Bissau	Yemen
Sierra Leone	Burkina Faso	Senegal	Yemen, Dem. Republic
Malawi	Angola	Mauritania	Bhutan
Guinea	Niger	Kampuchea	Nepal
Ethiopia	Central African Republic	Liberia	Bangladesh

past 25 years has outstripped world population growth by 25 percent. In the 1985 crop year, developed countries had grain surpluses totaling 182 million metric tons while developing countries had a deficit of 59 million metric tons. The United Nations estimates that world grain surpluses will total 384 million metric tons by the end of this year.

Still, most experts agree with Harl, who said: "We can give them food, but that has proven to be unwise in the long run. It's not the solution." In fact, there are no easy solutions, no obvious "mistakes" to point to. Nor are there easy ways to categorize hunger-stricken countries.

Brazil, for instance, has the Third World's richest store of prime farmland and natural resources. The country followed a rapid development strategy in the 1970s that many thought would conquer poverty and hunger by turning the South American nation into an agricultural-industrial giant.

Brazil has had some major successes. Today it is the No. 1 exporter of coffee and orange juice, the No. 2 exporter of soybeans and tobacco, No. 2 in producing cattle and cocoa, and No. 2 in corn production. It produces food in abundance, yet seven out of 10 people don't have enough to eat. Half of all Brazilian children suffer from malnutrition.

World malnutrition rates.

One in 10 children die before the age of 5, and the infant mortality rate in the impoverished northeast, home to a quarter of the population, is double the national average of 67 per 1,000.

There could be even hungrier times ahead, thanks to Brazil's staggering $121 billion international debt.

Development, paradoxically, has contributed to the problem. Concentration of land ownership has left 10.5 million peasants landless, most of them displaced by huge mechanized soybean farms, cattle ranches, and orange plantations.

Peasants have migrated to urban areas, where most live in poverty or have taken jobs as farm laborers for wages too low to provide an adequate diet for their families.

The search for causes of hunger turns up many similar contradictions:

☐ Overpopulation: Bangladesh, with an infant mortality rate of 124 per 1,000, is one of the most densely populated countries in the world. Mauritania, with an infant mortality rate of 132, is one of the most sparsely populated.

☐ Drought: Chad, with an infant mortality rate of 138, copes with perennial drought. Haiti, with an infant mortality rate of 123, is in a lush, tropical zone.

☐ Ideology: Tanzania, with an infant mortality rate of 111, is a Marxist country. Neighboring Malawi, with a mortality rate of 157, is capitalist.

"Malawi has chosen a capitalistic model of production and development. Tanzania has chosen an approach at the opposite extreme, a socialist approach. Neither approach has worked very well," said a relief official who has worked in both countries. "Malawi's development has categorically developed the western model—a good infrastructure, good roads, good airports, export-oriented agriculture, in the hopes that the benefits of development would trickle down to the poor. Tanzania has chosen the other way, a percolation from the bottom up."

☐ Foreign aid: Ethiopia, with an infant mortality rate of 152, receives very little development or economic assistance. Somalia, with an identical mortality rate, received $40.7 million from the United States alone last year.

Nevertheless, experts say U.S. aid is essential ammunition in the fight against hunger. There has never been a greater opportunity for an international effort to end hunger in every single country around the world, they say.

"Hunger can be ended," said Elizabeth Coleman, an official with The Hunger Project, a California organization devoted to ending hunger by the year 2000. "If people realize that, I think they will want to do something about it. It is not an impossible goal. The people in the suffering countries want to do something about it, but they need to have the economic ability to buy food. They need land to grow food."

2. Honduras

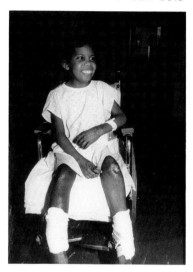

Maria del Carman Montenegro, 13, sits in a wheelchair in a Tegucigalpa hospital where she was treated for malnutrition and related ailments. Scars on her knees were caused by crawling around Tegucigalpa.

HONDURAS

Area: 42,300 sq. mi.

Population: 5.3 million

Population density: 125 per sq. mi.

Work force: 59% agriculture,
　　　　　　 21% industry

Literacy: 57%

Per capita income: $815/year

Life expectancy: 57

How Iowa compares:

Area: 56,290 sq.mi.

Population: 2.9 million

Population density: 52 per sq. mi.

TEGUCIGALPA, HONDURAS – Maria del Carmen Montenegro was destined for hardship before she was born.

Because of her mother's poor diet, Maria entered the world 13 years ago with partially formed, bent and twisted feet and legs. Poverty and her own poor diet of tortillas and beans continued the damage. The hunger-stunted child, who looks about 6 years old, cannot walk; bone-deep sores and scars caused by crawling city sidewalks mark her knees.

She is one of Honduras' many hungry children, hobbled by weak and broken bones, stick-thin limbs, poorly formed teeth, stunted bodies and parasite-bloated bellies. Their plight is a common one in Latin America, where control of land and resources by a small, elite class and a few large corporations has kept millions on the edge of starvation.

"Many people have the impression that there are few problems in Honduras because the country is not in the news that much," said Medea Benjamin, a Latin American expert with the Institute for Food and Development Policy in San Francisco. "However, it's the poorest country in Central America. It has the worst living conditions."

About 315,000 of the country's 702,000 children younger than 5 suffer from malnutrition; more than 86,000 are severely malnourished, according to a medical survey conducted by the Honduran government last year.

Of every 1,000 children born, 76 die before their first birthday and

116 die before age 5, according to the United Nations International Children's Emergency Fund. That means more than 81,000 of the 702,000 children younger than 5 probably will never reach that age.

Why so much suffering and death? It's hard to understand at first glance.

Despite drought in the south, Honduras has more than enough good farmland to feed its people. In fact, the country is a net agricultural exporter. Those exports totaled $650 million in 1986 while agricultural imports were just $71 million, according to the United Nations Food and Agriculture Organization.

But the country's prime farmland, where Indians once grew corn, beans and squash, is in the hands of foreign corporations or wealthy landowners who produce mostly export crops. Coffee plants cover the fertile highlands, while the best land in low-lying areas is used for bananas, sugar, cotton and grass-fed cattle destined for fast-food restaurants in the United States.

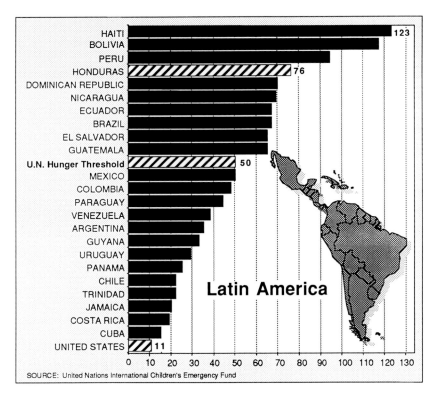

Latin America infant mortality rates. Deaths per 1,000 infants under age 1.

And that, said Patricia Ahern, is the root of the problem: Export profits benefit foreign interests and just a few privileged Hondurans.

"Land distribution and income distribution are the true causes of hunger in Honduras," said Ahern, who works with a peasant union here.

Foreign exploitation and the concentration of land ownership is a Honduran legacy dating back more than 400 years to the days of Spanish plundering, she and others said.

U.S. banana companies continued the legacy with their political and economic dominance beginning in the late 1800s. The companies still own or control large tracts of prime farmland in northern Honduras, where the best land is found.

"Bananas, sugar cane, pineapple, beef — it's all controlled by large landowners and foreign companies, and it's all for export," said Patrick Ahern, director of Catholic Relief Services here. "So the peasants have been forced into the hills, places you wouldn't even dream of planting crops. They are left with the worst land for domestic food products."

Ernesto Carbajal is one of those peasants. He, his wife and 11 children live in a wooden shack on a steep, rocky hillside in southern Honduras, where they try to grow maize on five acres of marginal land.

"The crop is ours, but the land is not," said Carbajal, 60. "I asked the owner to use it. Everything I grow, I get two-thirds. He gets the rest."

Rain has been scarce in the southern mountains, causing Carbajal's promising crops to wither and die before harvest.

"If I don't get anything, we both lose, and that's for the last two years. Not a single kernel.

"We don't have enough to eat. Some days we eat, some we don't. We've had about a year since we ate any meat."

Carbajal has considered joining the migration of thousands of rural peasants to Tegucigalpa, but he knows there are no jobs there. Instead, he and his oldest sons, ages 17 to 36, struggle to find work in nearby towns or with other farmers.

"We don't know what we are going to do," he said with resignation.

Paula Corrales, 48, is one who made the move to Tegucigalpa with her family, after struggling to survive on less than two acres in southern Honduras.

She and seven children, ages 3 to 19, live in a small shack atop a steep hill overlooking the city. She pays about $15 a month for the shack, which has no water, electricity, or even an outdoor privy. A father of some of her children, a day laborer, provides most of the family's income.

"We eat beans, tortillas and rice. We don't drink milk. There is not enough money," said Corrales.

Still, food prices are lower in the city, so her family is better off.

For most of this century, the major Honduran farmland owners have been from the United States – San Francisco–based Castle & Cooke Incorporated, producer of Dole brand bananas, and Cincinnati-based United Brands Company, producer of Chiquita bananas.

United Brands, which also owns John Morrell & Company, established its first United Fruit Co. operations in Honduras in the 1890s and was joined later by Castle & Cooke, which controls 170,000 acres of quality farmland, according to Oxfam America, an international development and disaster relief organization.

Ernesto and Altagracia Carbajal and seven of their children stand by their shack next to their cornfield in southern Honduras.

Experts say, however, that export cattle producers are now the country's dominant economic force in agriculture.

"If the best land isn't in bananas or sugar, it's in cattle," said Patricia Howard, a sociologist whose doctoral thesis examined Latin America's growing cattle industry.

The United States, looking for a cheap source of beef for its rapidly expanding fast-food industry, opened its import market for beef in the early 1960s, said Howard.

Prime Latin American acreage used for cattle grew rapidly with support from the World Bank, the International Monetary Fund, and the U.S. Agency for International Development. From 1960 through 1974, 60 percent of all World Bank farm loans to Latin America—$2.1 billion— went to cattle production. Beef production rose a whopping 750 percent.

In Honduras, land in pasture reached 8.4 million acres in 1980 from 4.9 million in 1960, or 65 percent of Honduran farmland. Just 22 percent is devoted to basic grains and "permanent" crops like bananas.

"Why is this important to hunger? One reason is the amount of land needed for cattle. You need one hectare [about 2½ acres] to raise a calf and about 1½ hectares to raise a full-grown one. If you increase your herd by 2 million head, you have to increase your pasture by at least 2 million hectares," said Howard.

Also, ranching is much less labor-intensive, she explained, "so cattle ranching translates into rural unemployment, rural-urban migration and displacement of food crops."

The result has been social, economic and ecological disaster in southern Honduras, where the Carbajals live. Hungry peasants are forced to the hills, where they practice "slash and burn agriculture" in a desperate effort to feed their families.

The southern mountains, once covered with dense green forests, have been denuded. Only patches of maize and a few stands of trees dot the steep, rocky hills.

And while the United States has pumped more food, development and military aid into Honduras, many experts say the aid, rather than improving conditions, has widened class differences and exacerbated hunger.

United States aid to Honduras has increased tremendously under the Reagan administration, rising to $190 million last year from about $30 million in 1980. Military aid was $61.2 million last year, compared with $4 million seven years ago.

"The United States is helping to create a civil war–type climate by providing aid without supporting agrarian reform," said Benjamin.

"U.S. aid is responsible for loads of dollars being spent in Honduras. Whether it is getting to the poor is questionable," said a U.S. embassy official who asked not to be identified.

Landless Hondurans can claim title to idle land under the country's agrarian reform law, so large landowners graze cattle as an easy way of using—and holding—the land.

Peasant organizations, frustrated by those tactics and the government's inaction, have tried to enforce the law on their own, occupying and making claims to 285 plots last year. The government recognized 36 of the claims and held others for "further study." However, it also arrested 450 peasants, while three were killed by landowners' guards.

As peasants struggle for land, Ministry of Health doctors continue their own struggle to save malnourished Hondurans.

Hungry, desperate Hondurans slash and burn vegetation and plant corn on steep hillsides.

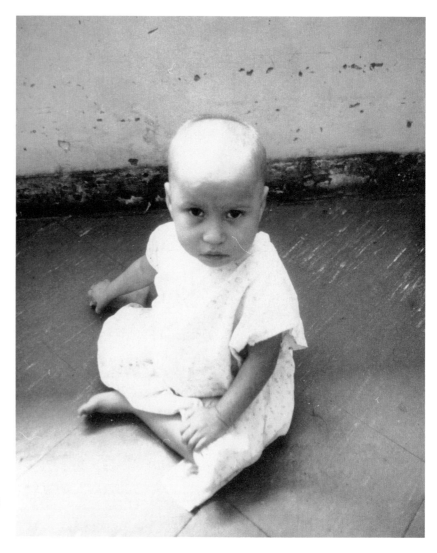

A child sits listlessly in a corridor of a hospital in Tegucigalpa, where she was being treated for severe malnutrition.

"The health budget was cut last year. We're spending more on weapons now and less on health and education," said a government doctor. "There's not even enough needles for penicillin shots."

Honduras has 200 hospital beds for the nation's 86,000 severely malnourished children.

"We have just 50 beds here in Tegucigalpa, and children get referred here from all over the country," said Dr. Juan Jose Nuvarro, a pediatrician who runs the public hospital nutrition ward.

"We basically save children's lives when they come here. Our mortality rate in the hospital is about 5 percent," he said, adding that hunger will continue until the economy improves.

"We can treat children while they're here," he said, "but we can't give their parents work. When they leave here, they go back to the same conditions they came from.

"The main factor is poverty, and that can only be addressed on a national level."

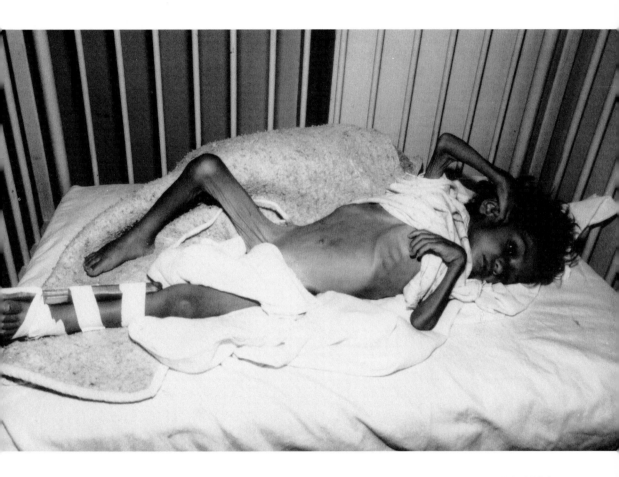

Malnourished Maises Banegas Anarriba, 3, rests in a Tegucigalpa hospital nutrition ward.

③. Ethiopia

MENDEFERA, ETHIOPIA—Father Paolos Fessehaie walked past rows of corn, potatoes, and onions, admiring the lush green patch they made in a brown scorched land.

Water has created a miracle near this Eritrean village. One small dam built with dirt and human hands has brought life to the people here.

"I remember when we dug this well," said Fessehaie, standing just below the dam. "It was nine meters deep to the water. Now the water is at the level of the land because of the dam.

"You can see, everywhere there are wells because of the dam. The soil is good, very good. It only needs water."

The water has allowed about 5,000 acres to be cultivated, supplying food and cash crops for about 25,000 people.

Still, abundance is the exception in this country. Hunger is the rule.

Famine, which claimed more than 1 million Ethiopians in 1984–85, is stalking again, threatening an estimated 6 million people.

Nine of Ethiopia's 14 provinces suffered drought and crop failures last year. However, drought is not the cause of hunger here. Hunger is an unnatural disaster caused by man.

Past feudalism, war, Ethiopian government policies, and the poli-

ETHIOPIA

Area: 472,000 sq. mi.

Population: 47 million

Population density: 100 per sq. mi.

Work force: 86% agriculture, 10% industry

Literacy: 15%

Per capita income: $110/year

Life expectancy: 39

How Iowa compares:

Area: 56,290 sq.mi.
Population: 2.9 million
Population density: 52 per sq. mi.

Father Paolos Fessehaie tells visitors he would like to see many more dams built like the one he is looking at near Asmara.

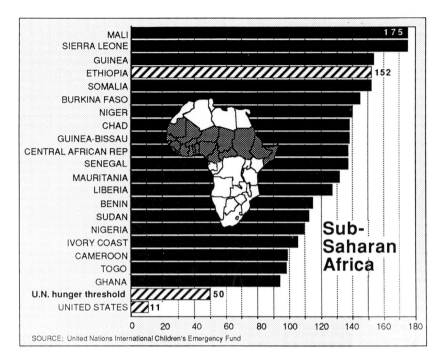

Sub-Saharan Africa infant mortality rates. Deaths per 1,000 infants under age 1.

cies of the United States and the Soviet Union all have had a role in the degradation of the land and its people. It's a formula for hunger common among dozens of African countries.

"Yes, there is a drought. But Ethiopia could be producing, even in drought years, enough food to feed everybody," said Joseph Collins, co-founder of the Institute for Food and Development Policy in California.

"They're going hungry because of a very military, top-down government with this very naive Marxist approach of shoving things down the throats of the people."

War in the provinces of Eritrea and Tigre has been shoved down the throats of Ethiopians for 26 years, first by U.S.-backed Emperor Haile Selassie, who annexed the former Italian colony of Eritrea in 1962, and most recently by Soviet-backed Marxist leader Mengistu Haile Mariam. Rebel forces are resisting what they consider an oppressive government.

When drought last year threatened to trigger another Ethiopian famine, relief agencies geared up quickly and were more than prepared to avert the catastrophe. Their efforts were disrupted, however, by major rebel offensives launched in April.

A bowl serves as the only marker for a Moslem grave in a cemetery of 1984 famine victims in Mekele, Ethiopia.

Ethiopian soldiers stand guard above a dam near Asmara in Eritrea.

Both sides have been accused of using starvation as a weapon—the Marxist rebels to swing world opinion to their side, the government to starve the rebels and their peasant supporters into submission. Mengistu has vowed to exterminate Eritrean and Tigrean rebels and has said there will be no economic progress in those provinces until he has done so. That could be some time. His forces have suffered major defeats this year.

An Ethiopian government food relief truck was blown up by rebels south of Asmara, killing the driver.

Mengistu "would just as soon see his country go down the tubes if he can't win the war," said one relief worker. "I don't think his concern for the people is that great. His concern is staying in power."

Ethiopians, meanwhile, are paying for the war with their lives.

At least 93 famine relief trucks have been destroyed by rebels; the government reportedly has burned fields and bombed villages; many emergency feeding centers have been closed in rebel-held areas, and most relief workers have been expelled from war-torn areas where people are almost totally dependent on emergency food.

Sehai Kiross holds charred wheat that burned for days after rebels attacked relief trucks in Eritrea.

"The tragedy, and I think both sides have to take some responsibility, is that they're escalating the conflict at a time when we should be escalating our relief," said Patrick Johns, director of Catholic Relief Services operations here.

Even without war, it would take years, billions of dollars in development assistance, and major government reforms to correct hunger-causing problems that originated centuries ago.

From 1916 to 1974, Ethiopia was ruled by the despot Emperor Haile Selassie. Wealth was concentrated in the hands of a few. There was almost no rural development, and peasants were forced to pay up to 75 percent of their crops as rent to feudal lords.

People desperate for food and fuel plowed pastures and stripped

People desperate for food and fuel stripped the highlands of trees, but plantings such as this one near the Mekele dam site may help.

the highlands of trees. In doing so, they unwittingly set in motion events that over time upset the ecological apple cart, turning their fertile farmland into dry wasteland.

The national forest cover declined from 40 percent in 1900 to just 4 percent today. As wood has become scarce, peasants have had to burn animal dung for fuel instead of using it for fertilizer.

The highlands, with 88 percent of the people and 95 percent of the arable farmland, are significantly eroded. An average of 168 tons of soil per acre are lost every year, rising to 240 tons per acre for cultivated land.

Mengistu's Marxist government, meanwhile, which overthrew Selassie in 1974, has continued repressive policies curbing peasant production.

Under Selassie, rich Ethiopians and foreign investors drove peasants off the best land and created big commercial farms and plantations for cotton, sugar and other crops.

Under Mengistu, most agricultural money goes to these plantations, now state farms. The farms provide food for Mengistu's army and produce crops for export to help finance the war.

Meanwhile, peasant farmers must sell goods to the government at low, fixed prices and pay hefty taxes for the war effort. With so much against them, they see little reason to produce more than they need for subsistence, even during periods of good rainfall.

Mengistu's policies have further dampened hopes for agricultural help from Western donors and lenders. The United States has spent hundreds of millions of dollars providing emergency famine relief but not a dollar for development.

"When the last emergency was ending in 1986, we pulled out. . . . We weren't going to have a long-range program in a Marxist country," said James Cheek, U.S. charge d'affaires in Ethiopia.

The United States and other Western nations are tired of bailing out the government with famine relief every few years, he added, explaining: "If things keep going the way they are, my grandchildren will be feeding millions of Ethiopians."

The World Bank, another Western-controlled institution aiding Third World development, ranks Ethiopia the world's poorest nation, with annual per-capita income of $110. It also says that per-capita development assistance here is the lowest in Africa—$9 per capita, compared with a sub-Saharan average of $18.

The bank identified potential food surplus areas—roughly a third of the country—in 1983 and drafted plans to increase production.

[Opposite] *In Ethiopia, Takel Abrha's wrinkled face reflects years of strife in her hungry country.*

Yet it has done little to promote agricultural development here, primarily because of Mengistu's farm policies. The government "opened the door a little" with a slight increase in farm prices earlier this year, said Michael Paison, the World Bank's director in Ethiopia. "So we're going forward with this [1983 plan] to see if we can ease the country's food problem."

Ignoring ideological disputes, private relief agencies are running several development programs. World Vision has helped Ethiopians transform a barren plain north of Addis Ababa into fertile cropland.

The Ansokia Valley plain, where thousands died of starvation three years ago, has topsoil 100 meters deep. The water table is down only two meters. World Vision officials say that with so much good soil and water, all the area needed was technical assistance and eager human labor.

Volunteers dig in the dusty earth in the Bet Ambessa dam site in northern Ethiopia.

So seeds, tools and oxen were given to 10,500 households. Irriga-

A worker stacks rocks at the Adi Alem (it means "New World") Dam site near Mekele.

tion systems were built. Banana, coffee, guava and papaya groves were planted.

Crops now cover the valley in community and family plots, expanding diets and offering new cash crops.

"Judging from progress to date," says a World Vision report, "the prospects for Ansokia as a drought-resistant pocket of paradise in the midst of a poor and troubled country appear highly promising."

Looking like a scene from the Bible, 1,700 Ethiopians work with their hands on the Adi Alem Dam. They are paid three kilograms of food a day.

There are other encouraging signs. Ethiopians in food-for-work programs sponsored by Catholic Relief Services completed 12 dams in Eritrea. Over 50 more are planned there and in Tigre. Eighty wells have been drilled in the two provinces, and 2.5 million trees have been planted.

About 1,700 people, each working for three kilos of food per day, are building a large dam near Mekele in Tigre, using only human labor to haul earth and rocks for the project.

The dam, sponsored by the Ethiopian Catholic Church, is being built with cooperation from the Ethiopian government and a local farmers' association.

"They make the people understand the necessity of the dam, and they accept it," said Father Gianni Premoli, a Mekele priest. "Now the people in all the small villages want to make their own small dams."

The potential is great. Sixty percent of Ethiopia's land is arable and only 10 percent is cultivated. The country has the ability to feed a population two to three times its size, U.N. officials say.

A mature green corn plant, with two ears showing tassels, grows in an irrigated field near Mendefera, Ethiopia.

But private relief efforts cannot keep pace with Ethiopia's problems. Not far from the Mekele dam, relief workers fight famine every day with emergency food and health care programs. Many people walk for up to a week and more than 100 miles for the food and health care.

"We see about 100 people a day," said Almuz Gabryseleic, an Ethiopian interpreter. "Malnutrition is the biggest problem. . . . They don't have enough to eat."

Food shortages have become so severe in Ethiopia that the threat of famine has become "a chronic condition; it can no longer be considered a cyclical phenomenon," says a report issued by the U.N. Emergency Prevention and Preparedness Group.

Efforts by relief organizations show what is possible on a larger scale, said Johns of Catholic Relief. But he said only high-level talks between the United States and the Soviet Union can end the fighting and allow large-scale development.

Parents wait with their children at the Latchi Health Clinic in Tigre Province, Ethiopia.

"These people are on the brink of an environmental disaster. The point is, something could be done about it, but the clock is ticking. We're past the 11th hour."

Ethiopians sit out the long wait for medical attention at the San Leopoldo Health Clinic in Mendefera. The posters on the wall above their heads show types of malnutrition in children.

4. Egypt

A child plays with pills she found in the garbage at her family's Cairo garbage village.

CAIRO, EGYPT–A filthy toddler atop a pile of garbage plays innocently with discarded containers of potentially harmful pills.

Not far away, her mother, Samira, and teen-age sister, Fayza, sort through the garbage for scraps to sell and food to eat.

Donkey carts filled with more trash rumble by, guided by children returning from the city.

All are from one of five "Zabaleen" communities in Cairo – about 100,000 people who pay for the privilege of collecting the city's garbage and taking it back to the dumps, or garbage villages where they live.

"I want for my daughter, the first thing, to be a daughter of Christ," said Samira, referring to her older daughter.

"And then, I want a better life, out of garbage, for my daughter. I don't know what she will do because she has no education, but I want a better life for her, out of garbage."

Samira's hopes seem reasonable on the surface, especially in light of the steady stream of U.S. assistance money flowing into Egypt.

But this is the country experts cite as a prime example of U.S. aid in the Third World run amok.

Egypt receives more U.S. food, economic and development aid than any country in the world except Israel – not because it is has the greatest need but because of its strategic importance in northern Africa and the

Middle East. Twenty-eight African countries have more serious poverty and hunger problems. But Egypt's bounty of U.S. food, economic and development aid exceeded the amounts received by all other African countries combined last year—about $1 billion, compared with $724 million for the rest of Africa. The country's $189.2 million in U.S. food aid alone was 36 times the $5.2 million provided to famine-stricken Ethiopia last year.

Still, only a small fraction of the food flowing into Egypt goes to

A toddler plays with discarded bottles of pills as an Egyptian woman and her daughters search for food to eat and scraps to sell in one of several garbage villages in Cairo.

EGYPT

Area: 386,650 sq. mi.

Population: 53.4 million

Population density: 138 per sq. mi.

Work force: 41% agriculture,
            14% industry

Literacy: 54%

Per capita income: $460/year

Life expectancy: 44

How Iowa compares:

Area: 56,290 sq.mi.

Population: 2.9 million

Population density: 52 per sq. mi.

Samira and other poor, hungry people. The rest, along with hundreds of millions in cash, is given to the government with no strings attached. Much of the grain goes to subsidize food prices for virtually all Egyptians, from the poorest to the most well-to-do. That gives U.S. officials pause. "It would be hard not to take a position that food ought to go to people who are hungry," a U.S. embassy official here said.

The official, who agreed to be interviewed if his name was not used, noted that the average Egyptian consumes 130 percent of the daily caloric requirement "while people in another country 500 to 600 miles away are starving."

At first glance, it doesn't make much sense.

"It's the politics of food," explained the embassy official. "To use it crassly for political reasons is hard to sell in the United States, to farmers in the Midwest. But I don't think there's been an administration since food aid was established that hasn't used it for political reasons."

A Government Accounting Office report says aid to Egypt is kept at a "high level for political purposes – peace in the Middle East."

"While Egypt does have substantial economic needs," it says, "the consensus of development experts . . . was that U.S. assistance to Egypt would range from $100 million to $200 million if it was based solely on relative economic need."

North Africa and Middle East infant mortality rates. Deaths per 1,000 infants under age 1.

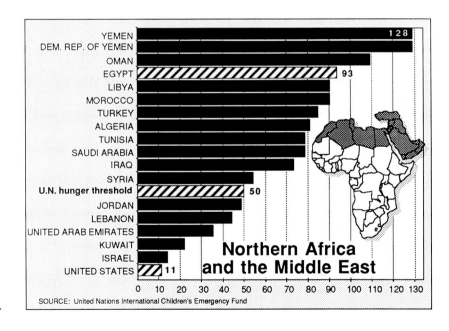

Four Zabaleen children arrive in their garbage village with a donkey cart brimming with garbage they collected in Cairo.

A Zabaleen girl drinks water from a faucet attached to a tank hauled into a garbage village in Cairo that has no running water.

[Opposite] *Abd El Metagaly in his wheat field north of Cairo.*

Despite all the U.S. food and economic assistance – $13 billion in 13 years – Egypt's economy is in turmoil.

Its agricultural sector, capable of producing enough food for all Egyptians, has been neglected and distorted by the government's cheap food policy to the point where Egypt has had to import about $4 billion in agricultural products in recent years. Even that hasn't been enough. The country is facing possible food riots this summer because of shortages and rising prices.

Also, while the average Egyptian eats very well, hunger is a fact of life for many.

The infant mortality rate is 93 per 1,000, almost twice the hunger standard of 50 set by the United Nations; 136 of every 1,000 children die before they reach age 5.

Mortality rates are at least that high among the Zabaleen, Christian farmers who migrated to Cairo in the 1940s to escape famine in southern Egypt.

Sanitation conditions in their garbage villages are abysmal. The newborn mortality rate was about 40 percent in Mokattam, the largest Zabaleen village, until volunteers established a clinic. "Now it is around 10 percent," said Dr. Adel Abd El Malek Ghali.

Experts say the government must shoulder much of the blame for

Full view of Abd El Metagaly in his wheat field.

Typical Egyptian bread made from wheat.

[Opposite] An Egyptian farmer rides a donkey loaded with clover to sell at market. He'll make more money than he would from growing wheat.

Egypt's food troubles. By following a cheap food policy that creates artificially low prices, the government has in turn discouraged food production. They add, however, that the United States has abetted Egypt. Instead of developing a solid agricultural base, U.S. food aid has helped take away the profit in producing food.

The government's policies have caused some "weird perversions" in the economy, according to Alex Rondos, director of Catholic Relief Services for the Middle East and North Africa. He noted that one-third of the best farmland is planted in clover because the state has set a low price for wheat and other grains but has not fixed the price of fodder.

"Clover is like gold," said Ahmed Bahgat, an agricultural expert. "From an acre of clover, you can get about 600 Egyptian pounds [about $267]. If you get three pounds [$1.33] from an acre of wheat, you count your blessings."

Agricultural price ceilings were eliminated last year, but subsidies will continue to depress the price of wheat and other grains.

An animal grazes in clover in Egypt's Nile delta, where many farmers grow clover instead of wheat and other food crops because of agricultural markets distorted by U.S. food aid and domestic economic policies.

As two farmers watch, a field of clover is watered by flood irrigation in the Nile River delta north of Cairo.

Food subsidies and guaranteed employment are a way of life for most Egyptians. "All university graduates are guaranteed employment. That means government work. So of the 25 million people of working age, 4 million are on the government payroll," said Rondos.

To keep so many on the payroll, the government keeps wages low—about $65 per month for a mid-level civil servant. It keeps the civil servants happy with food subsidies. In the process, however, Egypt has become a poor country.

With imports of more than $11 billion annually and exports of less than $4 billion, the government is faced with a $44 billion foreign debt it cannot service. It went to the International Monetary Fund for help last year and negotiated a $325 million credit and reform package.

Reforms have been instituted. Electricity rates have gone up 100 percent in more affluent neighborhoods, the price of bread has more than doubled, and sugar and cooking oil shortages have followed government belt-tightening.

Bahgat has felt the pinch.

Ahmed Bahgat, an agriculture expert, says Egypt's economic belt-tightening has affected his own middle-class family.

"We are upper-middle-class people, and it should not have affected us, but it has," he said, sitting in his comfortable suburban home discussing the painful economic restructuring.

"For us, a family of four, we used to eat a kilo and a half of meat [about 3.3 pounds] a week. Now my wife says a kilo is enough."

Yet Egypt has not phased out subsidies rapidly enough to satisfy the International Monetary Fund, which has delayed payments to Egypt under the credit package. Observers say the government is dragging its feet out of concern for the impact of austerity measures on the poor and because of fears of social unrest.

Ibrahim Nafeh, editor of the semi-official daily newspaper *al-Ahram*, earlier this year accused the International Monetary Fund of causing civil unrest in Argentina, Bolivia, Brazil, Ecuador, Haiti, Liberia, Peru, Sudan, and Egypt.

However, Rondos said, "I disagree with those who say the IMF is responsible. The country would have the same problems anyway. The government is going broke. They have survived for decades with a perverted subsidy program, and now they're having to pay their dues."

U.S. aid, meanwhile, helps shore up the government and its crumbling economy. In addition to the $185 million in food, about $815 million in cash was given to the Egyptian government last year.

"It's got to be one of the most corrupt countries on earth. You pump billions of dollars into a country, and you're asking for it," said Kevin Danaher, an Africa expert with the Institute for Food and Development Policy in San Francisco.

Corruption in Egypt is "institutional," said Rondos. "Money is fed into a bureaucracy, and that bureaucracy makes sure that money goes through it. It's a built-in corruption or inefficiency. Everything done here requires a committee." Unfortunately, poor Egyptians will have to pay the price for those inefficiencies.

"Life, even for the better-off people, is not what it used to be. So you can imagine what it means to the lower-income people," Bahgat said. "For many, it is very painful. For the majority, it is very painful."

5. Zimbabwe

SANYATI, ZIMBABWE – Piles of food dry in the sun outside the Gabatura family huts, creating a cornucopia of corn, melons, vegetables and peanuts.

"My life is getting better now. I'm getting happy," said Charles Gabatura, 40. "I have enough money to buy clothes and feed my family."

The Gabaturas have seven acres of cropland – four in cotton, two in

The Charles Gabatura family poses on their farm near Sanyati, Zimbabwe, with white maize and okra they grew drying in the sun.

ZIMBABWE

Area: 151,000 sq. mi.

Population: 9.7 million

Population density: 64 per sq. mi.

Work force: 25% agriculture,
22% industry

Literacy: 60%

Per capita income: $640/year

Life expectancy: 54

How Iowa compares:

Area: 56,290 sq.mi.
Population: 2.9 million
Population density: 52 per sq. mi.

corn, and one in peanuts. They eat the corn and peanuts and sell the cotton.

Having a cash crop and enough food for the family – including six children and a grandmother – is a new experience for Charles and Emma Gabatura. Until eight years ago, they and other small family farmers barely survived in good times and watched friends and relatives starve in times of drought.

Today, Zimbabwe stands as proof that a nation committed to fair distribution of wealth, food and land can make headway against hunger. However, it hasn't always been such an enlightened country.

"White explorers entered the area in the 1800s, looking for diamonds and other mineral wealth. Instead, they found rich farmland," said Robert Mazur, an Iowa State University sociologist who taught at the University of Zimbabwe for two years.

"White settlers, who made up about 5 percent of the population, took the best half of the land for themselves and pushed the Africans off into areas similar to the Indian reservations in the United States – poor land."

A lock on the most productive land allowed whites to keep blacks economically dependent, which created a low-wage labor pool for their commercial farms, mines and factories. "The result was tremendous poverty in black-held areas," said Mazur.

It wasn't malicious intent, just benign neglect, said Marvellous Mhloyi, a demographer and development expert at the University of Zimbabwe. "The white government, whether there was drought or hunger affecting blacks, that was not their concern. They just didn't care," she said.

Poverty, hunger, and the disparity in land distribution sparked a wave of black nationalism in the 1950s. Guerrilla warfare in the 1960s and 1970s brought the reluctant white regime to the bargaining table. Blacks gained independence April 18, 1980, and the country's name changed from Rhodesia to Zimbabwe, a Shona tribal name meaning "house of stone."

Dramatic changes followed, but not the ones the whites feared.

"People thought whites would be cut up, killed," said Robbie Mupawose, Zimbabwe's former secretary for the Ministry of Agriculture. "It never happened."

Instead, Prime Minister Robert Mugabe embarked on a program of reform designed to improve income and nutrition for the black majority. New minimum wages mean farm laborers who made as little as $3 a month in 1979 now are paid a minimum of $100 a month. The industrial

Robbie Mupawose, formerly secretary for the Zimbabwe Ministry of Agriculture, discusses agricultural and economic progress there.

minimum wage is $170. Zimbabwe has a nutritional monitoring system, and the new black government added emergency food programs to combat hunger in drought-stricken areas. Mugabe also established universal education and health care, and financed construction of community schools and health clinics throughout the country.

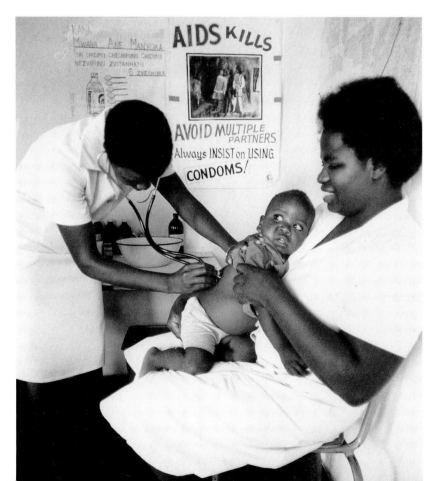

Unity Madhafi listens to Willard Siniwe's breathing as he clutches his mother, Anna, during a visit to the Murambwa Clinic in Zimbabwe.

Primary school enrollment rose to 2.3 million by 1985 from 819,000 in 1970. The number of schools jumped to 4,234 from 2,401 in that same period, and teacher ranks increased to 56,358 from 18,483.

About 1,000 students, mostly whites, attended the University of Rhodesia in 1980. Now, 7,500 students, most of them black, attend the University of Zimbabwe on the same campus in the capital city of Harare.

Equally dramatic strides have come in food production. Despite droughts in four of the last eight years, Zimbabwe not only has achieved self-sufficiency in its staple food, corn, it also has become an exporter to other African nations.

North of Harare stands one of the six cotton processing plants built in Zimbabwe during the 1980s. This one, built in 1984, can process 60,000 tons a year.

Black farmers, who grew 10 percent of the nation's corn prior to independence, grow 55 percent today. In 1985, small farmers harvested 1.8 million tons of corn, more than three times their previous output. The small farmers' share of marketed produce rose from 10 percent in 1980 to 38 percent in 1985, and the value of the corn and cotton sales grew from $17 million to $218 million.

Philemon Gwangwava, 55, is one of the farmers who has benefited. He lives in Zvataida, a farm community established on prime farmland

Farmers' co-ops in Zimbabwe towns give away brimmed seed-corn hats instead of billed caps familiar in the United States.

acquired by the government in 1981. His family and 26 others each were given 12 acres of cropland and 40 acres of grazing land.

"I have better crops and better grazing now. Last year I got 10 bales of cotton and 25 bags of maize. I have food and more cattle, and they are building a clinic just down the road. We think we are progressing well," said Gwangwava.

Under white rule, blacks grew just enough to feed themselves because they couldn't market products through official channels. Now, the new government has extended the agricultural support system established by Rhodesia for white commercial farmers to the black majority. The government, "in its wisdom," still supports white farmers, said Mupawose. It has purchased farmland for landless blacks only from farmers willing to sell.

But there has been more than land for blacks. Roads have been improved in black farming areas. Distribution centers for seeds, fertilizers, pesticides and tools have been established. Grain storage depots and crop collection points have been built, and the agricultural extension staff has been increased to help boost small-farm production and net income.

[Opposite] *Farmer Amos Mutidu wears a straw cowboy hat to the Sanyati cotton terminal.*

"We encourage the use of hand tools and ox-drawn plows," said Mupawose. "Everyone wants to run machinery, but there are problems. On small farms, it is very expensive."

The Gabaturas live less than a mile from a paved road and a new depot where they buy cotton seed and sell their harvested cotton. The depot, opened in 1984, is next to a new cotton plant capable of processing 60,000 tons per year. It is one of six such plants built since 1980, bringing the country's total to eight.

Marketing boards buy farmers' products at prices that guarantee them a profit, and village stores are stocked with food, clothing and other items.

"Rural development has been essential," said Mupawose. "It is futile to have good agricultural programs without rural development. If farmers have money and nothing to buy, what is the incentive?"

Credit from the government's Agricultural Finance Corp. has been important, too. A United Nations report on Zimbabwe says the farm lending policy is "the single most important factor in raising small farmers' yields. . . . In 1985, the government loaned about $35 million to

Like a scene in the American Midwest, a grain elevator stands at the edge of Chegutu in Zimbabwe.

Thousands of bags of cotton seed are stored at the Cotton Marketing Board's Sanyati depot.

90,000 small farmers, compared with $1 million that went to fewer than 4,500 small farmers in 1979."

However, problems remain:

☐ The mortality rate—110 deaths per 1,000 infants in 1960—was still at 76 per 1,000 in 1985, according to U.N. figures. Mhloyi said the

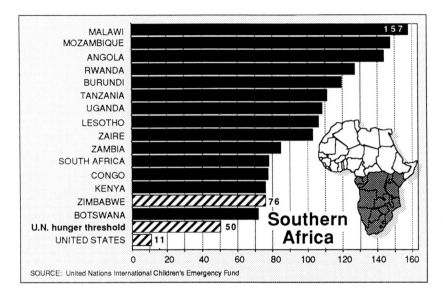

Southern Africa infant mortality rates. Deaths per 1,000 infants under age 1.

rate has been cut to 60, still above the U.N. hunger threshold of 50.

☐ Ambitious plans to resettle black families in the first three years of independence were scaled back because of budget constraints and a shortage of white farmers willing to sell good farmland. About 60,000 families have been resettled, while 900,000 families remain on poor, dry land.

☐ Zimbabwe's population is growing faster than its economy, fueling fears of rising unemployment just as secondary school and college graduates' expectations are rising. Each year 100,000 blacks graduate from high school and enter a job market with room for 7,000.

☐ The country is starved for outside capital.

Most observers say Mugabe is a brilliant, pragmatic populist who has followed policies in the best interests of the Zimbabwe people. Nevertheless, he describes himself and his government as Marxist. That, plus instability in southern Africa, has cooled Western investment. The United States slashed aid by nearly half after Mugabe's government chose to differ with Washington on several U.N. votes. The remaining aid was halted last year after a Zimbabwe official criticized U.S. policy toward South Africa.

Zimbabweans say South African aggression and economic destabilization is the biggest problem for all countries in southern Africa. In addition to arming guerrillas, sometimes with U.S. help, South Africa has directly attacked nine of its neighbors, including Zimbabwe, and has tried to assassinate two prime ministers, including Mugabe.

While Zimbabwe spends $784 million a year for education and $262 million for health care, $720 million is spent defending borders and vital rail lines.

The United Nations International Children's Emergency Fund estimates that South Africa-sponsored terrorism has cost southern Africa's black states more than $25 billion since 1980. More importantly, hundreds of thousands of people have been killed or have died in war-caused famines.

Mhloyi said most people in southern Africa believe the United States is indirectly supporting South Africa's disruptive activity.

"The way people perceive war here is that it is the giants fighting in Africa. They have to fight some way, and so they're doing it through the people of Africa," she said.

"If you give us peace, all you need to do is give us agricultural aid for a short time and we can take care of ourselves. This is what we say in Zimbabwe. Give us peace."

⑥. South Korea

SUWEON, SOUTH KOREA – Lee Minjae steps outside his farmhouse and grabs a bucket with one hand and a rag with the other and heads for the barn. It's time for evening chores, and Lee is about to pump cash in the form of milk from his 15 Holstein cows.

Miles away in the modern urban capital of Seoul, consumers flock

Farmer Lee Minjae gets ready for evening milking of 15 Holstein cows on his dairy and beef farm near Suweon.

to Lotte Center, a glittering 14-story department store including restaurants and a modern supermarket filled with meats, dairy products, fruits, vegetables, and packaged foods.

Lee, with his dairy herd and 30 beef cattle, is in an enviable position — poised to take advantage of South Korea's booming economy and the rising consumption of meat and dairy products sold in shops like Lotte Center.

The United States takes a share of the credit for South Korea's economic transformation. U.S. development aid has worked wonders here, working in tandem with new government policies designed to distribute wealth and foster prosperity for small family farmers. Food and hunger experts say that while South Korea still has serious political problems, its successful agrarian reforms are a showcase for what can be accomplished in developing countries.

South Korea has achieved much more than simple agricultural reform. Without a doubt, the country is basking in economic prosperity.

South Koreans shop for breads and pastries in a downtown Seoul supermarket that also is full of meat, milk products, fruits, and vegetables. Rising income put more variety in Korean diets.

The country – one of Asia's four "little tigers" along with Taiwan, Hong Kong, and Singapore – generated real economic growth of more than 12 percent last year and has enjoyed an average annual growth rate of more than 10 percent in the last five years.

Annual per-capita income, approaching $3,000, is rapidly increasing, although farm income has lagged in recent years. The average rural household makes about $7,000 per year while the average urban household makes about $12,000, giving South Korea the largest middle class in Asia outside Japan.

The rising income has led to a higher standard of living, a more varied diet, and an end to serious hunger problems and food aid.

The infant mortality rate, the most widely accepted hunger measurement, has dropped from 85 deaths per 1,000 infants in 1960 to 27 per 1,000, well below the 50 per 1,000 hunger threshold established by the United Nations.

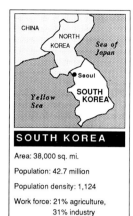

SOUTH KOREA

Area: 38,000 sq. mi.

Population: 42.7 million

Population density: 1,124

Work force: 21% agriculture,
31% industry

Literacy: 93%

Per capita income: $2,849/year

Life expectancy: 67

How Iowa compares:

Area: 56,290 sq.mi.

Population: 2.9 million

Population density: 52 per sq. mi.

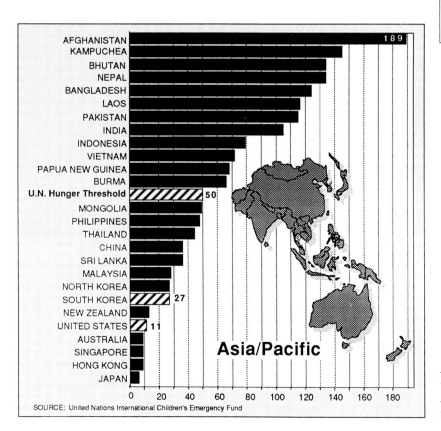

SOURCE: United Nations International Children's Emergency Fund

Asia/Pacific infant mortality rates. Deaths per 1,000 infants under age 1.

And while South Korea has increased its own agricultural production, it also has become an important market for U.S. farm products. Thousands of bakeries have been built, spurring the import of U.S. wheat, and feed grain imports have grown as meat and dairy consumption has increased. In the last 15 years, annual per-capita beef consumption has almost tripled to eight pounds from less than three pounds, per-capita milk consumption has jumped to 70 pounds from 5½ pounds, poultry consumption has increased to seven pounds from four, and pork consumption has increased to 20 pounds from six.

"I think Korea is probably the best example of a country in which nutritional improvement has translated into food demand," said Neil Harl, an Iowa State University economist who has studied South Korea's development. "It is an example of a country which has come from a devastated economy to an emerging, vital economy in a fairly compressed amount of time."

South Korea's history until recent decades had been a story of hunger. Feudal lords ruled for centuries, exploiting peasants and keeping all of the land and riches to themselves. Japan occupied and exploited the country's resources and people from 1910 until the end of World War II.

The country's troubles continued after the war, with the partitioning of the country into a Soviet-dominated north and a U.S.-dominated south. Then Communist North Korea invaded in 1950, and the south was all but destroyed by the three-year war. For the rest of the 1950s, North Korea progressed with Soviet help while South Korea languished.

"Farmers were absolutely poor and hunger was widespread," said Park Sang-woo, director of South Korea's agricultural policy bureau. One important step had been taken, however: The South Korean government had enacted sweeping reforms putting land that had been controlled by feudal lords and the Japanese in the hands of peasant farmers, who made up more than 80 percent of the population.

"That was a very good thing because in rural areas we established a very equitable society," said Lee Nai Soo, director of research for the National Agricultural Cooperative Federation. "There is no big shot in rural society. Everyone is the same."

In 1961, an army coup brought Gen. Park Chung Hee to power. Park, with U.S. assistance, launched economic development programs designed to improve agricultural production and the quality of life in rural areas. "Eradication of hunger was a top priority. We should be emancipated from hunger," said Park Sang-woo.

Then in the 1970s, two critical factors accelerated the pace of

Chung Moo Nam of South Korea's Rural Development Administration next to high-yielding rice plants.

change. "New high-yielding varieties of rice were developed, and the government launched a national community development program," said Park Sang-woo. "The combination brought a 'green revolution' to Korea."

South Korea, a densely populated country with limited farmland, doubled agricultural production from 1962 to 1977, achieving self-sufficiency in rice, its staple food crop. At the same time, farmers thrived because of rural community development, technical assistance, financing for seed and supplies and crop price supports.

As recently as the late 1970s, farm income was higher than average income for urban manufacturing workers. Even today, small family farmers are protected with price supports and a law that bars any farmer from owning more than 7½ acres.

But with people well fed and thriving on their farms, the stage was set for industrial development. It began in the 1970s with textile and assembly operations. Wages were low and social services poor as the government poured most of its resources into industrial development and promoted a "sacrifice for national progress" philosophy.

Aspirations have risen in recent years, however, as South Korea has become more industrialized. The population is now 80 percent urban, and South Korea has graduated to heavy and high-tech industries—steel, autos, electronics, computers.

Workers demanding a greater share of the rapidly growing wealth staged violent strikes across the nation last summer and again this year, winning pay raises averaging 20 percent. Overall, consumer incomes have increased by 40 percent over the past two years.

A South Korean government publication says the country was slow to start public welfare programs, "but as many sectors of society were exposed to the ill effects of rapid industrialization and as a growing need was felt for an improvement in the distribution of wealth, medical aid and other welfare projects have been expanded at a fast pace."

The government intends to have the entire population covered by a medical insurance program by the 1990s and has enacted a national pension law that will provide old-age, disability and survivor benefits.

Meanwhile, workers' growing incomes have nurtured a rapidly growing market for U.S. agriculture. South Korea has become the third largest importer of U.S. agricultural products behind the Netherlands and Japan, said James Ross, a U.S. embassy official representing American agricultural interests here.

Agricultural imports increased by 24 percent last year, reaching

$4.2 billion, primarily because of increased demand for hides and feed grains. U.S. farm imports increased 41 percent to $2 billion. Feed grain imports have risen to more than 7 million tons from 600,000 tons in 1975, with the U.S. share up to 4.5 million tons.

"Per-capita meat consumption is still very low, so I expect to see much more livestock production," said Lee Nai Soo. "That means much more imports of feed grains, which is good news for the United States."

Like their counterparts in neighboring Japan, South Korean officials remain very protective of their farmers. The small size of family farms, which helped the country distribute land and income in earlier years, is putting a strain on farmers today.

"Everything is couched in farmers being a very traditional part of the society," said LaVerne Brabant, director of the U.S. embassy's agricultural trade office. "They are seen as a very weak group that needs to be protected at all costs."

While trying to preserve that philosophy, a protective barrier banning imported beef has provoked a bitter trade battle between the United States and South Korea. U.S. officials insist that the South Korean government must relax the ban while the Korean government and farmers here say the U.S. demand is unreasonable.

"You ask us to import your feed and you ask us to import your meat. That would destroy everything," said Lee Shil-kwan, a farm cooperative official. "We import your feed to produce the pork, the beef, the poultry. That is the way it should be."

Despite these difficulties and differences, it is agreed that South Korea is rapidly emerging from developing to developed status. The very fact that the United States is willing to fight for greater market access is a reflection of that success.

"Korea is a country with a future, and American agriculture has a great future here," said Brabant. "We don't have a consumer movement here yet . . . but time is on our side. Korea is going to move much more quickly than Japan. The population is going to put pressure on the government for consumption."

The development of South Korea's agriculture, the subsequent industrial development, and the growing market for U.S. products hold an important lesson, according to Harl.

"The surest route to development for all Third World countries is to help them improve their agriculture, to help them do better what they're good at doing, producing food," he said. "Critics say that is a foolish approach. We'll only make them competitors. But that is a short-term phenomenon."

Ross added: "If Koreans hadn't developed their industry to the extent that they can sell Hyundais in Iowa, they wouldn't be in a position to buy Iowa's corn and soybeans."

7. Third World Debt

A PESTILENCE has infested the world, spreading hunger, misery, and death: Third World debt.

At $1.2 trillion and growing, the debt is more widespread and potentially more devastating, experts say, than the effects of drought, locusts, and all other natural disasters combined. It is sucking the life-blood out of many Third World countries, said Susan George of Paris, author of "A Fate Worse Than Debt."

"Over $130 billion net–repayments minus new loans–has left Latin America and landed in Northern banks in the past five years alone," she says in the book, which was published in April.

The United Nations International Children's Emergency Fund says debt and economic measures imposed to deal with it are eroding the health and nutrition of children in Africa and Latin America. The agency calls debt an "opposing force" to child survival.

Steps to curb the mounting debt are sapping the earning power of many in the Third World. UNICEF says average incomes fell in 17 out of 23 countries in Latin America and in 24 out of 32 countries in sub-Saharan Africa between 1980 and 1985. Overall, average incomes fell by 9 percent in Latin America and by 15 percent in Africa.

"Stagnating trade, falling commodity prices, declining aid, mounting debt repayments and a steep drop in private lending have stalled economic development in many countries during the decade," says UNICEF. As a result, many nations are faced with spiraling debts and severe balance-of-payments problems, and approximately 70 countries

Third World debt.

have had to turn to the International Monetary Fund for assistance.

But the International Monetary Fund doesn't offer easy solutions. It requires economic "adjustment policies" as a condition for assistance, and those measures inevitably hit poor, hungry people the hardest, George said in an interview.

"The IMF, when it comes in and starts managing a country's economy, says two things: 'Earn more. Spend less,'" she said.

"Earn more means export more. That means cash crops, to the detriment of food production and the local economy. That means a drop in commodities prices in world markets and lower income from exports."

The "spend less" side of the equation means cutbacks in government health, education, and welfare budgets, particularly food subsidies. UNICEF says government spending on health and education has declined in half the nations of Africa and Latin America during the 1980s.

In addition to those measures, the International Monetary Fund also pushes for a devaluation of the nation's currency to foster more exports, which means everything imported costs more. The net result, said George, is that food prices rise and employment and per-capita income decline, compounding severe hunger problems just when public nutrition, health, and other social services are being cut.

"We are starting to see polio coming back in Jamaica because the government can't afford vaccinations. Malaria is coming back in many countries because they can't afford to spray for mosquitoes," she said.

UNICEF reports that low birth weights and child deaths are on the increase in Barbados, Belize, Bolivia, Brazil, Chile, Jamaica, the Philippines, Uruguay, and in several financially strapped African countries. The organization says it doesn't question the need for adjustments that will lead to restoration of economic growth, "but UNICEF does question whether it makes either human sense or economic sense to sacrifice the growing minds and bodies of the next generation on the altar of adjustment policy."

UNICEF sees alternatives to the IMF adjustment formula. First, the organization wants a commitment on the part of a nation's leadership—and the international community—to protect the poorest individuals while working to restore economic growth.

"From that commitment, for example, can flow policies which favor the small farmer and small producer in order to improve employment, productivity and incomes and nutrition among the very poor," it says.

Zimbabwe's recent successes in food production, UNICEF notes, are largely a result of investing in the productivity of the poor themselves. "Similarly, such a commitment could also lead to a restructuring of government spending to favor low-cost basic services for the masses rather than high-cost special services for elites."

For example, the government of the Philippines in the last year of the Marcos regime spent about five times as much on four sophisticated hospitals as it did on primary health care services for the whole nation, UNICEF says.

In contrast, Indonesia boosted spending on immunization and still cut total health spending, simply by postponing construction of new hospitals. The international community, for its part, needs to put more emphasis on debt rescheduling, improved aid, increased lending, and greater access to rich markets for poor countries' goods, says UNICEF.

Iowa State University economist Neil Harl said international lenders could learn a great deal by looking at the experience of farm lenders, who eventually reached the conclusion that debt restructuring was the best course for both farmers and lenders.

"We restructured farm debt, forgiving principle and interest payments in many cases," said Harl. "We need to do the same thing with the Third World. There is an enormous capacity for lenders to broker losses that cannot be paid. Everybody takes a hit, including lenders who are not exposed.

"We have to start eating that debt. . . . If we don't, we'll continue moving toward a cataclysmic event. It's likely, if we keep the screws tight, that we will pay for it in serious social unrest."

Or, as UNICEF sees it: "No adjustment policy is acceptable which allows children to be sacrificed for the sake of financial stability. Yet this has happened, and it need not happen. Alternatives exist."

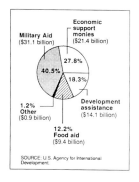

World distribution of U.S. aid, 1981-1986.

8. A Search for Solutions

ADDIS ABABA, ETHIOPIA—There is a saying among the people here: "The Russians bleed us. The Americans feed us."

Ethiopians don't want to be bled. They don't want to be fed. They want to feed themselves. Yet Soviet military support for an unpopular civil war has been bleeding them for years, and American food aid—withheld some years and extended in others—has kept them teetering on the brink of starvation. So while Russians are viewed with derision, Americans are viewed with suspicion.

These feelings toward the superpowers, common among people in the Third World, go to the heart of the world hunger debate. Why are Third World people being bled to the point that 18 million die of hunger every year? Why are 1 billion—more than ever before—chronically hungry?

U.S.-Soviet wrangling is part of the problem, and food and hunger experts are quick to offer other reasons. But answers also can be found among the people themselves.

Ernesto Carbajal, a Honduran peasant, knows he's forced to farm and go hungry on a steep, rocky hillside because the rich and powerful of his country control the valley to raise cattle for fast-food hamburgers.

Father Paolos Fessehaie, an Ethiopian priest, knows his neglected people are starving and dying while his government wages war and the United States and the Soviet Union fight for dominance in Africa.

And Lee Minjae, a South Korean farmer whose ancestors knew

nothing but hardship, knows he has land, livestock, and prosperity today because sweeping reform and rural development, backed by U.S.
aid, gave land and income to hungry peasants.

These Third World people carry a message, say the experts: People
need the chance to fend for themselves.

"For hungry people, opportunity can mean many things: access to
education, health care and family planning services; credit and loans to
enable them to improve their land or purchase land; effective transportation, marketing systems and storage facilities; jobs to generate income
sufficient to purchase food," says a report by The Hunger Project, an
organization dedicated to ending hunger by the year 2000.

Neil Harl, Iowa State University economist and organizer of the
1988 world food conference in Des Moines, sees hunger in a similar
light. "First and foremost, I think hunger is caused by low income, the
inability of poor people to demand the food they need," said Harl. An
extended drought can upset food flows, and war and economic destabilization can cause hunger, too.

"I tend to think, however, that the most pervasive problem is lack of
income. Even with drought, if people have money, they can buy the food
they need," he said.

People won't have the money, however, unless they are given the
power to earn it, said author Susan George, a hunger expert. "I see
hunger very much in terms of power relationships. I always have," she
said. "Food is a source of great wealth and power. With hunger, very
often it's a situation of, 'If I win, you lose.' If one person has good land,
another doesn't."

Joseph Collins and Frances Moore Lappe, co-founders of the Institute for Food and Development Policy in San Francisco, said people's
power must come from basic democracy—an accountability to the people by governments, corporations and other powerful interests. Lack of
accountability can be found in both right- and left-wing governments,
and even in the way the superpowers use countries as pawns in their
own power struggles, they said.

"I'm against any ideological, doctrinaire approach, especially when
it's combined with an attitude that it doesn't matter how many people go
hungry, as long as we get our way," said Collins.

In Ethiopia, the Marxist government, the United States, and the
Soviet Union are playing power games at the people's expense, Collins
added.

"It's an overall mindset, whether it's in Ethiopia or the Philippines," he said. Government leaders gain "a false sense of security" by keeping a heavy hand on the people.

Lappe also noted that big U.S. food corporations, which made $4.7 billion on sales of $115 billion last year, could earn even more if they would abandon the notion that they have to exploit Third World people to make a profit.

Big food companies have collaborated with oppressive governments and wealthy landowners in countries around the world, she said, adding that she has seen the results firsthand in the Philippines, where peasants' crops have been bulldozed by powerful plantation owners producing fruit for Nabisco Brands Incorporated and Castle & Cooke Incorporated.

"Companies are being incredibly shortsighted by resisting change in the Third World. If there was a process of income redistribution going on in the Third World, the demand for many products would soar," said Lappe.

The United Nations Children's Fund says there is another faulty mindset—an "out of date" attitude that it is "normal for more than 14 million of the world's young children to die every year and for millions more to live in malnutrition and ill health."

Poverty and hunger can be wiped out, says UNICEF, but it will take major reforms, including land reform and economic policies that give the poor more clout and a fair chance to earn a living wage.

That goal has been met in some developing countries. In China, Taiwan, and South Korea, agrarian reforms have given people the land, the resources, and the farm income to survive and even thrive. Infant mortality rates in all three countries are well below the hunger level established by the United Nations.

"China was a country that had widespread famines for years and years," said Collins. "They were blamed on drought or overpopulation or whatever. But the real cause was the nation's feudal system."

Giving people the tools to end hunger, however, often meets with strong opposition from powerful interests. Land reform in Latin America, for instance, has been brutally resisted. In Brazil, despite a land reform law, millions of small farmers have been pushed off their land to make way for mega-farms benefiting large corporations and wealthy landowners. Two percent of the farms occupy 58 percent of the farmland, and the richest 1 percent of the people hold as much national wealth as the poorest 50 percent.

In 1985-86, land barons had about 500 Brazilian peasants and peasant supporters killed after the people sought enforcement of the land reform law. With such powerful forces working against hungry people, what else can be done?

Harl said a first step should be a Third World Marshall Plan, a development aid program on the scale of the effort made to rebuild Europe after World War II. U.S. economic aid to Third World countries today ranks last among 17 industrialized countries in terms of percentage of gross national product, and less than one-tenth of what it was as a percentage of GNP under the Marshall Plan.

"For a country with our wealth and capacity, our aid level to the Third World is a disgrace," said Edward Schuh, dean of the Hubert Humphrey Institute at the University of Minnesota.

Harl added: "This is so important to our security that a portion of the assistance ought to come from defense."

Experts also say there will have to be major reforms in aid programs because U.S. aid has been guided more by political factors than by effectiveness or need.

"Clearly, we have retarded progress by propping up right-wing types and prolonging their influence," said Harl. ". . . There are Marxist regimes badly in need of aid, but the U.S. government can't see its way to provide them assistance, and so we push them into the arms of the other side."

Schuh said aid in most cases should zero in on agricultural research and improving rural health care, schooling, nutrition, and development. "If countries don't have policies that allow effective use of aid, then I don't think we should give it to them," he said. "In too many cases," added Shlomo Reutlinger, an official with the World Bank in Washington, "we're giving aid without asking for some development benefit."

World Bank official Robert Armstrong said the bank in recent years has focused on requiring needy countries to reform food policies that aren't constructive. The goal is to give farmers the prices and resources needed to increase food production and income, he said.

He acknowledged that the bank has been criticized for emphasizing export crops at the expense of food crops that can be consumed by a nation's own people. But he defended the policy, explaining, "In many cases, the countries that have done the best in export production have also done the best in food production. These are not mutually exclusive areas. Export production and food production are often complementary and improved by the same policies."

Susan George said one way to avoid aid pitfalls would be to channel more food and development assistance through private relief agencies working directly with peasants "to get the resources to the people who need them."

However it is achieved, agricultural development remains the key to progress in most developing countries, said Harl. "Raising people's incomes is essential," Harl observed. "In the beginning, that usually means increasing food production."

Boosting agricultural production in the Third World should pay off for U.S. farmers, too. John Block and Bob Bergland, former U.S. secretaries of agriculture, said in a recent *Register* article that the Third World offers the greatest growth market for U.S. agriculture.

"U.S. farm leaders sometimes worry that if those millions of poor farmers are trained and encouraged to produce more, American agriculture will not be able to compete. We argue the opposite: If those millions of poor in the Third World are able to develop their economies and thus be part of the economic mainstream, American farmers will have a sales opportunity far beyond their expectations," Block and Bergland wrote.

While a few big corporations and wealthy individuals may profit from hunger in the short run, George added, ending hunger would benefit almost everyone in the long run:

"In the industrial north, we're losing jobs because we can't sell our goods to Third World countries. In the Midwest, our farmers are struggling because we can't sell them our agricultural commodities.

"Everybody is losing."

II. Made in Mexico

THE FOLLOWING SECTION contains a series of
articles about foreign-owned plants in Mexico
called "maquiladoras." At the time of the series'
publication in 1986, there were roughly 750 such
plants employing 260,000 workers. These workers,
one expert said, moved "perilously between destitution and mere subsistence, even while surrounded by the glitter of 'progress.'"

The "glitter of 'progress'" she referred to continued from 1986 to 1989. There were 1,500 maquiladoras employing 370,000 workers by the end
of 1988. Most of the plants were owned by U.S.
companies that had migrated to the border area to
take advantage of the extremely low wages on the
Mexican side. But others were there, too—plants
owned by companies based in Taiwan, Korea, and
Japan—and the explosive growth was continuing.
Experts estimated that there would be 1,750 maquiladoras employing more than 430,000 workers
by the end of 1989. Some expected there would be
3 million Mexicans employed in maquiladoras by

the year 2000. "Oh man, it's fantastic!" said one maquiladora booster.

The growth of "glitter," however, had not been accompanied by similar progress in wages and living conditions. Workers were making just over $4.00 a day when I was there in 1986. By 1989, their wages had eroded with the value of the peso to less than $3.70 a day. Many Mexicans working 48 hours a week in maquiladoras found it more difficult to feed their families in 1989 than they did in 1986. And an estimated two-thirds of Mexico's population was suffering from some form of malnutrition in 1989, up from one-half in 1982.

There was a relative bright spot, however. Employees with an unusually strong worker organization in Matamoros, just south of Brownsville, Texas, had managed to negotiate higher wages and a 40-hour work week for workers in maquiladoras there. Wages for workers there were roughly $5.70 a day in 1989.

"Everyone was saying, 'Since the workers are getting a little more and are working decent hours, all of the maquiladoras would move away.' Well, they've roughly doubled since you were here," said Ed Krueger. The American Friends Service Committee official said the number of maquiladoras in Matamoros had grown to 72 employing 31,000 in 1989 from 36 employing 22,000 in 1986.

"The little more companies are paying workers in Matamoros hardly shows on their bottom line," he said. "We're not talking about a difference between $15 an hour and $20 an hour. We're talking about a difference between 50 cents an hour and 75 cents an hour.

"I think it's ridiculous when these companies try to trim the wages down to such low levels. It hurts the workers, and it hurts the companies in the long run because the workers have bitter feelings. When the workers have bad feelings, their quality of work is not as good."

⑨. The Migration of Jobs

TIJUANA, MEXICO – Sanjuana Orrdaz works 48 hours a week to feed her children dinners of tortillas and atole, a hot drink made of flour, milk and water. This Tijuana woman, who labors for 50 cents an hour for the Mexican subsidiary of Iowa's Ertl Company, says she is happy to have a job and a roof over her family's head, but the money "is not enough."

Her story is repeated thousands of times south of the border by employees who work in U.S.-owned plants called maquiladoras, collecting Mexico's minimum wage of about $4 a day. The workers "move perilously between destitution and mere subsistence, even while surrounded by the glitter of 'progress,'" contends Maria Patricia Fernandez-Kelly, a maquiladora expert with the University of California at San Diego.

More than 1,300 miles away, Rose McNaughton of Sioux City, Iowa, a former Zenith Electronics Corporation worker, bitterly remembers when her $5-an-hour job migrated to Mexico in 1978. "They took more than a paycheck away from us. They took a way of life," says McNaughton.

Orrdaz and McNaughton are the products of an explosive trend that began in the mid-1960s, when U.S. corporations, feeling the threat of international competition, began shifting production and jobs in significant numbers to Mexican border cities. In some cases, the maquiladoras have meant the difference between corporate failure and survival. "If we

---

Register Staff Writer Lou Ortiz assisted in the reporting for this article.

were not in Mexico, there would not be a Zenith," said Vince Kamler, Mexico operations manager for Zenith Electronics Corp., one of the largest maquiladora employers.

The trend also has driven millions of dollars into border city economies, and employment in the export-oriented Mexican plants has grown in quantum leaps, more than doubling in the past five years.

Today there are more than 700 factories stretching 2,000 miles along the border from Tijuana near the Pacific Ocean to Matamoros near the Gulf of Mexico, employing more than a quarter of a million workers in what has become one of the fastest-growing—and lowest-paying—industrial corridors in the world.

The value of goods manufactured in these border plants has increased more than 700 fold during the past 20 years, with the biggest growth occurring in the past two to three years. And it's not over yet. In

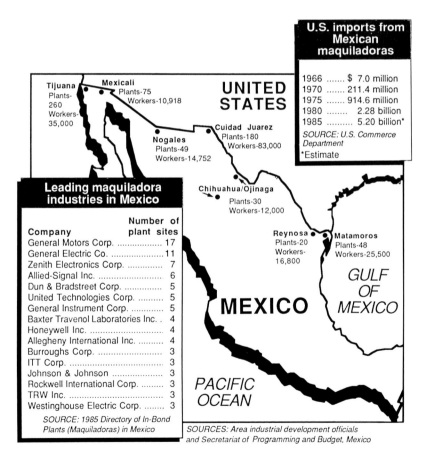

Number of plants and workers in major maquiladora cities.

U.S. imports from Mexican maquiladoras

1966	....	$ 7.0 million
1970	....	211.4 million
1975	....	914.6 million
1980	....	2.28 billion
1985	....	5.20 billion*

SOURCE: U.S. Commerce Department
*Estimate

Tijuana Plants-260 Workers-35,000
Mexicali Plants-75 Workers-10,918
UNITED STATES
Cuidad Juarez Plants-180 Workers-83,000
Nogales Plants-49 Workers-14,752
Chihuahua/Ojinaga Plants-30 Workers-12,000
Reynosa Plants-20 Workers-16,800
Matamoros Plants-48 Workers-25,500
GULF OF MEXICO
MEXICO
PACIFIC OCEAN

Leading maquiladora industries in Mexico

Company	Number of plant sites
General Motors Corp.	17
General Electric Co.	11
Zenith Electronics Corp.	7
Allied-Signal Inc.	6
Dun & Bradstreet Corp.	5
United Technologies Corp.	5
General Instrument Corp.	5
Baxter Travenol Laboratories Inc.	4
Honeywell Inc.	4
Allegheny International Inc.	4
Burroughs Corp.	3
ITT Corp.	3
Johnson & Johnson	3
Rockwell International Corp.	3
TRW Inc.	3
Westinghouse Electric Corp.	3

SOURCE: 1985 Directory of In-Bond Plants (Maquiladoras) in Mexico

SOURCES: Area industrial development officials and Secretariat of Programming and Budget, Mexico

one area of Tijuana, more than 30 new factories are under construction right now.

The growth has been fueled by the enormous wage differential between Mexico and the United States, by the proximity of the area to major U.S. markets and by Mexican and U.S. tariff provisions that encourage corporations to move jobs across the border.

The economic and sociological impact of all this, on both the U.S. and Mexico, has been enormous. In the United States, tens of thousands of jobs, including more than 1,500 in Iowa, have been lost. In Mexico, border cities have become clogged as tens of thousands of workers have migrated from interior cities, accepting living conditions that sometimes are unsanitary.

Most maquiladoras are labor-intensive electronics and textiles enterprises, but other industries also are discovering the advantages of Mexico's cheap labor. Some of the operations are small sweatshops above run-down storefronts, but many are technological marvels, housed in sprawling industrial parks. Once the employees don factory garb and take their place on the assembly line, the setting could be any modern industrial plant in the U.S.

Maquiladoras are owned by some of the world's largest corporations: General Motors, Zenith, Texas Instruments, Mitsubishi, Honeywell, Sony, Chrysler, GTE, Mattel, Sanyo, RCA, and others. The power of these plants was brought home to Iowa in 1978, when Zenith closed its plant in Sioux City and moved more than 5,000 U.S. jobs to Mexico and Taiwan. The Sioux City plant, which had employed more than 3,000 workers in the early 1970s, was the town's largest employer−1,500 workers at the time of the closing.

Other Iowans have been affected, too. Three Iowa-based companies now employ more than 5,000 Mexican workers, embracing the low-wage, low-cost climate along the border: A.C. Nielsen Clearing House, a Clinton coupon-processing subsidiary of Dun and Bradstreet Corporation; Ertl, the Dyersville-based toy manufacturing subsidiary of Kidde Incorporated, and Winegard Company, a Burlington electronics firm. Winnebago Industries Incorporated of Forest City opened a sewing operation in Ciudad Juarez last year but closed it after six months because of "internal management problems" and sluggish recreational vehicle sales.

Industrial development officials predict, however, that many Midwest companies, including some in Iowa, will recognize the advantages of maquiladoras and will establish permanent operations south of the border in the future.

"That guy with the toy company in Iowa didn't go to Tijuana just because he thought it was a neat idea. He did it because of what the global market dictates. Industries are having to go where they can find the lowest-cost labor," said Teri Ritter Cardot, a vice president with a southern California firm that helps companies establish Mexican operations. Cardot said that auto-related industries—considered important to Iowa's industrial future—have been following U.S. auto makers to Mexico in recent years. General Motors, Ford, Chrysler, and American Motors all have Mexican plants that export cars or components back to the U.S.

Defenders of the movement of jobs to Mexico from Iowa and other states say it has been a boon to workers in both countries. It has provided sorely needed jobs in Mexico, where an estimated 40 percent of

In a climate-controlled room in a Zenith plant in Reynosa, Mexico, young women peer into microscopes as they install electronic components. They work for about $4 a day at jobs Iowans used to perform for $5 or more per hour.

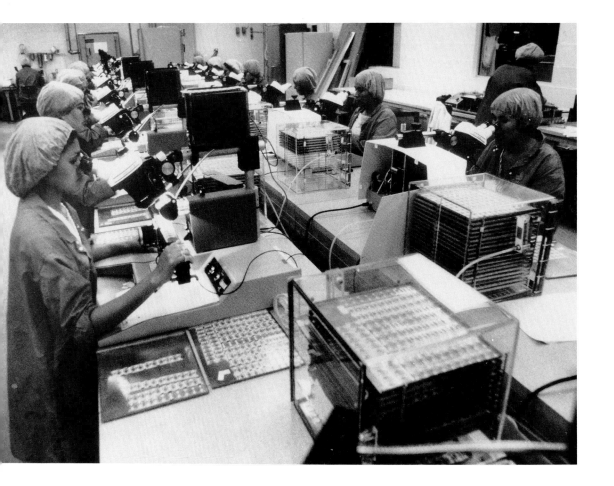

the people were either unemployed or working at whatever jobs they could find – even before the country's petroleum industry was buffeted by declining world oil prices. And it has allowed U.S. companies to survive in today's competitive world markets, preserving other U.S. jobs.

Critics say, however, that maquiladoras create more problems than they solve. In the United States, opponents say jobs are being taken from Americans, and employees of corporations with major Mexican operations say the threat of job losses hangs over their heads. "Our management keeps telling us, 'We gotta do better.' We have to do this or that, or they're going to move. It's always the threat," said Karlene Bass, who works at a Zenith plant in Springfield, Missouri.

In Mexico, the radical changes triggered by the maquiladoras' expansion have caused problems along the border. City services and housing can't keep pace with the growth in population, and the sudden rush of young women into the work force is causing social upheaval.

But while there is strong disagreement about the plants' virtues and vices, almost everyone agrees that wages in these factories, among the lowest in the world at $4 to $7 a day, have propelled the growth in this border region.

Even Japanese and other foreign companies are beginning to discover the Mexican border area and are forming American subsidiaries to take advantage of the low wages and tariff breaks available there. Those tariff breaks include U.S. and Mexican customs provisions that allow companies to ship parts and raw materials into Mexico duty-free. Then the assembled components or finished products are shipped back to the United States with tariffs paid only on the "value added" to the products, based on Mexico's low labor rates rather than on the market value of the goods.

While the maquiladora program, originally limited to the border area, has been expanded to virtually all of Mexico, most companies still locate along the border for transportation, communication and other reasons, including the opportunity for American managers and their families to live in U.S. cities.

The success of this program simply oozes from official statistics. The U.S. Commerce Department says the dollar value of exports to the United States from Mexican maquiladoras has grown from $7 million in 1966 to $211.4 million in 1970 to $2.28 billion in 1980 to an estimated $5.20 billion in 1985.

Just 64 plants employing 22,000 people dotted the border in 1970. During the early 1970s, however, the number of maquiladoras grew at an annual rate of more than 30 percent, pausing briefly during the 1974–1975 recession, when about a third of the 80,000 workers lost their jobs. Growth resumed in 1976, and by 1980 the Mexican border area had become the cheap-labor assembly capital of the world, outpacing its Third World competitors with 420 plants and almost 100,000 jobs.

But that was just the beginning. During Mexico's economic crisis in 1982, the peso suffered a 600 percent devaluation—from 25 pesos to the dollar to 150.

For the maquiladora workers, it became a disaster as daily wages plunged to about $4 a day from $11 the year before. But it gave Mexico a tremendous labor-rate advantage over most other Third-World countries.

In 1984, for instance, the total hourly cost of an unskilled worker in Mexico ranged from 65 cents to 94 cents, compared with an average $5.90 in the United States, $2.30 in Hong Kong, $1.40 in Taiwan and $1.81 in Jamaica.

A few Caribbean and Central American countries have lower hourly labor costs, but those countries do not have the transportation and inventory advantages provided by a common border with the United States. Mexico also offers U.S. corporations a reasonably stable political climate. Thanks to those factors and others, the number of maquiladoras increased to 745 by the end of 1985, with total employment rising to 260,000 from 100,000 in 1980.

The maquiladoras now make up the second-largest source of foreign currency for Mexico, surpassing tourism, bringing in about $1.4 billion last year. Only petroleum, which brought in an estimated $14.6 billion, ranks higher. Experts say they expect world economic conditions to remain favorable for maquiladora growth, and they "conservatively" estimate that by the end of 1995, there will be 1,500 to 1,800 plants with at least 1 million workers, earning $10 billion for Mexico.

Community officials on both sides of the border are scrambling to accommodate the growth that has taxed roads and community services. A streamlined commercial crossing has been opened to speed the flow of truck traffic near an industrial park east of Tijuana. Thirty plants are under construction there, and a one-stop maquiladora service facility is rising on the U.S. side.

Officials in the El Paso-Ciudad Juarez area are pushing for a large commercial bridge spanning the Rio Grande. The bridge would be designed to handle heavy truck traffic and would rekindle that area's maquiladora boom, they say. Other border towns are eying similar bridge and industrial park plans as competition for plants intensifies.

[Opposite] *Reynosa, Mexico. Dozens of young women peer into microscopes in the quiet, dust-free environment of this lab. They are placing (with vacuum and mechanical aids) minuscule electronic parts in place.*

Maquiladora: A history lesson

Maquiladora is derived from the Mexican word *maquila,* or *maquilar,* which in colonial Mexico meant the income earned for processing someone else's grain. Mexican farmers took their grain to millers for processing *(maquilar)* but continued to own the grain after the millers' labor and services were completed.

Similarly, foreign companies own the parts and raw materials they ship into maquiladoras and continue to own the finished products after the Mexican workers' labor has been added to its value.

Maquiladoras also are called "twin plants" because U.S. companies frequently have operations on both sides of the border. However, most experts say the label is a misnomer because companies typically have their labor-intensive production on the Mexican side, with just administrative offices, warehousing, and transportation facilities on the U.S. side.

They're also called "in-bond plants," because U.S. corporations or American subsidiaries of foreign companies must post a bond in Mexico ensuring that the products made from parts and raw materials shipped into Mexico are shipped back out of the country.

A company may be allowed to sell up to 20 percent of its maquiladora production in Mexico if there are no Mexican competitors making the same product. The U.S. company also may be required to use an established percentage of Mexican parts and raw materials in the finished product.

The rush to the border began 20 years ago after the Mexican government launched its "Programa de Industrializacion Fronteriza," or maquiladora program, in hopes of providing employment for thousands of migrant workers left jobless when the United States terminated the International Agreement on Migratory Workers.

That agreement, better known as the "Bracero Program," was established in 1942 when there was a wartime shortage of labor in the United States. It allowed millions of Mexican workers to enter this country and was continued after the war because of its popularity among produce growers and other businesses employing Mexicans at low wages. Finally, in 1964, Congress ended the program, leaving about 200,000 Mexican workers unemployed.

Mexican officials had hoped the maquiladora program would absorb unemployed male migrant workers and help alleviate poverty and unemployment along the border. From the beginning, however, the arriving multinational companies have preferred to hire young women, typically between the ages of 16 and 24. About 80 percent of the workers are young women, officials say.

"Instead of solving a problem, the program brought a new group

American industries don't have to go far across the border to take advantage of the low-priced labor in Mexico. The streams of motorists who cross the heavily traveled bridge over the Rio Grande between El Paso, Texas [left] and Ciudad Juarez [right] can see a large industrial park [top], which contains many maquiladoras—production plants owned by U.S. companies.

into the work force and created new problems," said Moises Sandoval, editor of a magazine published by the Catholic Foreign Mission Society of America.

Researchers at the University of Texas at El Paso, the University of California at San Diego, and El Colegio de la Frontera Norte, which has offices in several Mexican border cities, generally agree with that view, saying that the maquila program has had limited success in attaining its stated goals:

☐ Easing the severe unemployment problem along the border.

☐ Earning sorely needed foreign exchange.

☐ Providing labor experience and training for skilled work with modern technology.

☐ Allowing the effective transfer of technology.

Nevertheless, the Mexican government in recent years has promoted and nurtured the program "as an emergency measure to assuage the ravages" of the country's severe economic crisis, says Fernandez-Kelly, the maquiladora expert at the Center for U.S.-Mexican Studies at the University of California at San Diego. "There is no question that the maquilas have benefited the Mexican economy, and the money is benefiting Mexican nationals. If they didn't have those jobs, they probably wouldn't have jobs," said Oscar Martinez, director of the Center for Inter-American and Border Studies at the University of Texas at El Paso.

Nevertheless, Martinez and other professors at the university have concluded that the program has not reduced border unemployment. Professors Edward George and Robert Tollen found in their studies that the maquiladoras not only have failed to reduce unemployment, they "may, in a sense, aggravate the unemployment problem" by attracting waves of migrants from the interior.

Exact unemployment figures are not available, but the men said in their February 1985 report that unofficial estimates of unemployment range from 25 percent to 40 percent, "and underemployment is a serious problem in the existing work force." Migration to the border also is causing severe housing, sanitary and other service problems for Mexican border cities as populations explode and as primitive "colonias," or housing developments, sprout with just the barest of services. It's not unusual for maquiladora workers to live in houses that are little more than shacks, with no sanitary sewers and frequently no water.

Experts add that the entry of women into the work force is causing social upheaval in Mexico's male-oriented society. "It's breaking up the family. The man in Mexico is supposed to work. The woman is supposed to stay home. That is a very strong tradition there. So the men start drinking. The women stop listening to them because they're making the money, and marriages become very unstable," said Sister Alicia Salcido, a Catholic nun who spent two years working with maquiladora workers in Ciudad Juarez.

Finally, critics say there has been a direct adverse effect on maquiladora workers, who work long, tedious days for little pay, sometimes in hazardous conditions, under pressure to increase production. "For the young people, this is easy money for a while. They just accept the conditions, but to see all the exploitation . . . it makes me so angry. To me, it's just slavery," said Salcido.

Maquiladora experts say it's hard to gauge what the impact has been in the United States. George and Tollen found that unemployment rates in many U.S. border cities have been substantially higher than the national average in recent years, despite the influx of maquiladora enterprises. And some companies along the border have followed the lead of their Frost Belt counterparts in moving operations to the Mexican side of the border. Farah Mfg. Co. Inc., for instance, has moved thousands of jobs from its home base in El Paso to Ciudad Juarez.

Workers crossed out "U.S.A." and penciled in "Mexico" on a giant poster at the Zenith Electronics Corp. plant in Springfield, Mo., after some production was moved to Mexico and the plant's employment plunged to 1,100 from 4,200.

10. Better Life, Low Wages

One processes coupons. Another makes toys. The third makes electronics gear for televisions. They have little in common, except for two things: Nielsen Clearing House, the coupon processor; Ertl Company, the toy maker; and Winegard Company, the electronics manufacturer, are all based in Iowa, and they've all moved some of their operations to plants in Mexico to take advantage of low labor costs.

Workers at the Ertl plant in Tijuana, Mexico, finish their lunch break by tossing around a volleyball on the loading dock.

TIJUANA, MEXICO – The white block factory sits at the foot of a hill, in an area where humble houses and shacks crowd in with dilapidated stores and makeshift businesses. Large block letters proclaim its identity: Ertl de Mexico, the Mexican subsidiary of Ertl Company, a Dyersville, Iowa, toy company best known for its metal miniature replicas of tractors, combines, disks and other farm implements.

Register Staff Writer Lou Ortiz assisted in the reporting for this story.

"When I first came down here, seeing all the poverty, I really felt sorry for the people. But you do get a little callous. You can't help it," said H. H. "Bud" McFadyen, operations manager for Ertl here, as he drove through a neighborhood near the plant. Driving by some shacks, he said: "I hope they [Ertl employees in Mexico] live a little better than that."

Ertl's employees, like most maquiladora employees, do live better than the thousands of squatters in the Tijuana slums. Most can afford four solid walls and enough food to stay healthy.

Single young women living with their parents can afford even more—nice clothes, jewelry, and occasional nights on the town. Most maquiladora workers in their late teens and early 20s, in fact, dress up for their factory work: dresses, heels, jewelry, makeup.

Yolanda Martinez, 24, an Ertl "lead lady" (assembly line supervisor) who lives at home with her mother, father and little boy, said the work at Ertl is good and the pay is adequate for women such as herself who live

H. H. "Bud" McFadyen, Ertl de Mexico plant manager.

Tijuana, Mexico—A maquila worker Jesus Gama loads cases of plastic toys bearing the Dyersville company name in Ertl's warehouse. Ertl officials used the Tijuana plant as a lever during labor negotiations in Iowa.

at home. But "for the girls who are heads of households, it's tough on minimum wage," she said.

The minimum wage in Tijuana and other border cities went up 32 percent in January, increasing to 11,550 pesos for a 48-hour week, or 1,650 pesos per day based on seven days a week. That comes to about 241 pesos an hour, or about $4 for an eight-hour day. Martinez makes an extra $11.11 a week as a "lead lady."

Ertl, a subsidiary of New Jersey-based Kidde Incorporated, bought its plant in January 1984 to test the advantages of those rock-bottom wages after Revell Incorporated, another toy and hobby kit company, decided it wanted to sell "because it was not running profitably," said Tom Conry, Ertl's vice president for administration. The move seemed wise, said Conry, because other toy companies have been shifting production to Mexico and cutting prices.

Tonka Corporation, based in Minnetonka, Minnesota, moved about 800 jobs from Minnesota to El Paso-Juarez a few years ago, he said. "They were strong competition to begin with, but that move made them a very formidable opponent because their prices dropped 25 percent to 40 percent almost immediately," Conry said.

For Ertl, "the experiment has been largely successful. The labor rate, as you know, is substantially lower, and there is an abundance of good Mexican nationals to work with," he said. Conry said it's never been Ertl's goal to move production from Iowa to Mexico. Rather, the idea has been "to augment our operations, which should increase our business in Dyersville."

Nevertheless, Ertl officials last March used the Tijuana plant – where plastic toys, kit parts, and children's record players are made – as a lever during negotiations with the local United Auto Workers union in Iowa. Company President Fred Ertl, Jr., warned that the company would shift production to Mexico unless workers went along with labor contract revisions.

"Because of the union's adamant and seemingly foolish stand, we will be forced to proceed with plans to outplace work that would have been done by Dyersville temporary and permanent employees to Mexico, other U.S. sources, or the Far East," Ertl said in a letter to employees. Ertl had asked workers to allow the company to increase its hiring of temporary workers during peak production periods from 20 percent to 50 percent of the regular full-time work force, a proposal rejected by union members in January 1985.

Ertl has about 800 full-time employees in Dyersville, including 550

[Opposite] *Maricela Perez Suarez, 20, who has four children, works in the Ertl plant in Tijuana. Even at minimum wage, the jobs afford many young working mothers a better style of living.*

production workers who make about $7 an hour. Benefits add another $2.30 to hourly labor costs, Conry said. The company argued that it needed to be able to hire more temporary workers at $3.50 per hour, with no benefits, to remain competitive and to guarantee the security of the permanent work force in Dyersville. The union, however, "had some concerns about job security and Ertl's intentions to stay in Iowa," said Conry.

The company agreed during subsequent negotiations to adopt provisions to protect full-time workers from layoff when temporary workers are hired, and union workers have agreed to allow Ertl to hire more temporary workers, with the number increasing to 425 from 290 during the three-year contract ratified last month.

"It was a question that we either agree or we wouldn't have any jobs. So we agreed," said UAW official Don Grimes. "They told us that our jobs would be moving unless we gave them the right to hire more temporary employees. We had no choice but to go along."

The work force in Tijuana fluctuates, too, but the company doesn't have to worry about asking for permission to hire temporary workers. It's a non-union plant. Last year, the work force ballooned to 225 while Ertl de Mexico was making plastic cars for McDonald's Corporation, then dropped to 85 when the job was finished. "We made 8.5 million of those cars. That's a lot of little cars to make in five months," said McFadyen.

He and the Tijuana plant's quality control manager, Rick Savedra, agreed that wages are very low in Mexico, but he said Mexicans and

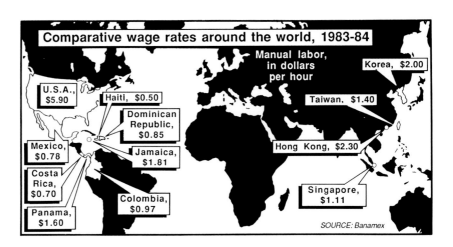

Americans would be worse off without the maquiladoras. "Maybe the wages are too low, but I don't set the wage. The government sets the wage. The Mexican government knows that companies go where they get the most for what they pay," Savedra said.

CIUDAD JUAREZ, MEXICO – The announcement capped two decades in which jobs trickled slowly out of Clinton, Iowa, south to this Mexican border town. Nielsen Clearing House, a Clinton-based division of A.C. Nielson Company, said in January that it would close its Clinton coupon-sorting operation, a fixture of the economy there since 1956, and eliminate about 100 jobs. The company will keep about 600 management, professional, clerical, and marketing jobs in Clinton, but the labor-intensive task of sifting through millions of coupons each month will rest solely in the hands of Mexicans once the latest transfer is completed later this spring.

Jay Bristol, an A. C. Nielsen vice-president.

Nielsen isn't new to Mexico. "We came here very quietly 20 years ago to take advantage of the lower costs of doing business," said Jay Bristol, a Nielsen vice president assigned to the company's office in El Paso, Texas, just across the border from Ciudad Juarez. "You have to go where you can get the least expensive fingers and toes to sort the coupons, and we have some very good ones. We can be very selective. There are plenty of people to choose from."

Nielsen's "fingers and toes" are a bargain in Ciudad Juarez, where many workers earn less than $4 for eight hours of work. Nielsen provides attendance bonuses, transportation, a cafeteria subsidy, and a savings plan to which the company contributes 10 percent of each worker's pay. Nevertheless, labor costs are extremely low. Bristol describes Nielsen's operations there as "wall-to-wall girls sorting coupons." Turnover is very high, he added, "because of the boring nature of the work." Many of the young women sit and sort coupons all day at well-worn tables in straight-backed wooden chairs. Some now use IBM personal computers. The company has 120 personal computers in Ciudad Juarez and has ordered 65 more.

Nielsen started with a small operation in Nuevo Laredo, opened a larger one in Ciudad Juarez, a third in Chihuahua and a satellite operation in Delicias, south of Chihuahua. Gradually, the company has become one of the largest maquiladora employers south of the border. The subsidiary of Dun and Bradstreet Corporation now employs 4,800 workers in four Mexican cities and has a fifth small plant in Port-au-Prince, Haiti.

A Nielsen Clearing House employee in Ciudad Juarez, Mexico, just across the border from El Paso, Texas, sorts coupons for which she is paid about $4 a day. A company official describes the plant as "wall-to-wall girls sorting coupons." Turnover is very high "because of the boring nature of the work," he adds.

The company sorts and processes coupons for about 200 retail chains and 2,000 individual retailers. It also sorts, counts, and statistically analyzes coupons for about 800 manufacturers interested in coupon effectiveness. "We are the leader. We have about 30 percent of the clearing house business. The next largest has about 15 percent," said Bristol. And the next largest, as well as others in the business, also call Mexico home base. "All of our coupon competitors are right here. . . . They all followed us," he said.

Nielsen's move to Mexico gave the firm a competitive edge, but Bristol says there were other critical reasons: "We've got to keep costs down to keep the program attractive to manufacturers. They will stop using coupons if the costs of handling run too high. If we don't have coupons, we don't have business, so it's more of a survival thing than a competitive thing."

Bristol said the move to Mexico hasn't stolen jobs from Clinton. "Clinton couldn't support this," he said, during a plant tour in Ciudad Juarez. "There aren't enough people. We have enough trouble finding people for the jobs we have there."

The coupon industry has grown 80 percent in the last four years and is expected to grow another 10 percent this year because coupon processors have kept costs in line, he said.

MATAMOROS, MEXICO – Officials of Burlington, Iowa-based Winegard Company say they hadn't planned on anything big, "just a little feeder plant," when they opened their maquiladora here in 1972. Beginning with just 10 workers, however, the company has gradually added products and employees to its Winegard de Mexico subsidiary. Today, Winegard employs 115 people and makes video selector switches, FM stereo antennas, amplifying devices and other electronics components at its Matamoros plant. "We opened the plant here because we were getting clobbered by Far East companies," said Michael Wales, Winegard de Mexico's general manager. "What we're really down here for is to take care of the labor-intensive things."

Low wages and other advantages of the Mexico location have let the company remain in business without having to buy products and components from Far East manufacturers, said Wales, a Burlington native who now lives in Brownsville, Texas. He contended that the Mexican operation hasn't cost any jobs in Iowa because "we wouldn't be building this stuff in Iowa. We would be sourcing it from somewhere. The market would dictate that." Mexico, he said, "is very competitive in

*Juarez, Mexico—
"121, 122, 123,
124"... an A. C.
Nielsen worker
counts coupons.*

the world labor market today. The communication, the transportation
and inventory carrying costs are all advantages, too, because we're just
across the border from the United States. If you have a shipment in the
middle of the Pacific and you decide you don't need it, it's kind of hard to
stop it.

"Haiti's got a tremendous program. Their wages can compete with
anybody's wages in the world. You give them a chicken head and a bowl
of soup and they're happy. But there again, you have the water connection."

Workers at Winegard de Mexico and other workers in Matamoros
work just 40 hours a week, instead of the standard 48, and are paid
more than most workers because they have a relatively strong local

union here. Standard pay is 16,392 pesos a week, or $34.50. The wages include pay for Saturday and Sunday if attendance is perfect. Workers are not paid for missed days, and their weekend bonus is reduced if they miss work.

While wages paid to workers will remain stable between now and January when wages are renegotiated, he said, "I know the peso is not going to be stable during that time," which means Winegard's labor costs will go down during 1986. "The bottom line is what you're getting out of 'em," said Wales, who runs the plant with his wife, Lydia, a Mexican-American who has worked off and on for Winegard de Mexico for the last 12 years. Lydia Wales, a Brownsville native, handles union negotiations, banking, schedules, and other administrative matters.

Many of the workers in the plant have the monotonous task of working on circuit boards, soldering wires, or dipping amplifier boards in hot pots of soldering liquid. The plant has production standards, Wales said. Male supervisors "measure each girl on each job." However, the production standards at the Matamoros plant are no more stringent than standards at Winegard's plants in Iowa, he said. "When production transfers down here, the standards transfer with it. The only difference is, we pay incentive in Burlington and we don't here." The Matamoros plant is one of five operated by Winegard. Three others, employing 160 workers, are in Burlington and a fourth, with 60 workers, is in Chariton, Iowa.

Officials said the Iowa workers' wages are about five times higher than Winegard workers' wages in Mexico, but the company has no plans to move more production to Mexico. "Our posture here is to make as much as we can in Iowa. We don't want to buy offshore, so we're doing everything we can to keep costs down. In order to compete, we had to do something," said Gene Dubrosky, Winegard's vice president for manufacturing in Burlington.

11. Sanjuana

TIJUANA, MEXICO—The days start early for Sanjuana Orrdaz, a 40-year-old woman who works for survival at a plant owned by the Ertl Company of Dyersville, Iowa. She's up at 5 a.m., and it's still dark in winter when Sanjuana leaves her four children and her humble three-room dwelling in the steep, unstable hills on the outskirts of town. Once at work, she will spend at least eight hours a day making toys that her own children will never have.

She is the sole provider for the family. And despite her relatively low wages, the money she brings home means the difference between eating and starving for her four children.

Orrdaz is one of thousands of Mexicans, many of them young women, who have found employment in the maquiladoras, the U.S.-owned assembly plants that are sprouting all along the border.

It's a long journey from Orrdaz's home to the Ertl factory. The walk she takes to the nearest highway—down rutted roads and a precipitously steep path—is treacherous when it's dry and almost impassable when it rains.

At the bottom of the hill, she takes a shuttle downtown. From there, she and other workers catch another taxi to the industrial park where Ertl de Mexico manufactures toys.

The trips to and from work take three hours each day and cost Orrdaz 320 pesos, almost 20 percent of her daily pay of 1,650 pesos (about $4). So she smiled and welcomed a ride at the end of a recent work day.

The ride with a reporter, a photographer and an interpreter began in Tijuana's rush-hour traffic, creeped to the city's freeways, and finally reached a remote area of unstable soil, rocks and mud slides, where many of the city's working poor live in small, tenuous dwellings.

Orrdaz talked about her work and life along the way. She likes her job at Ertl, she said through interpreter Francisco Bernal, a publications translator for a government-funded research center in Tijuana. The money she makes is welcome but "isn't enough." Orrdaz, who helps assemble plastic toys and children's record players for Ertl, makes 11,550 pesos (about $25) for a 48-hour work week. Employees doing similar work in Ertl's Dyersville plant make anywhere from $3.50 to $7 an hour, depending on whether they are full-time union employees or temporary workers.

Her weekly paycheck is parceled out for necessities: 1,600 pesos ($3.37) a week for transportation to and from work, 4,000 pesos ($8.42) for food, 4,000 pesos for bottled water and 1,000 pesos ($2.11) for electricity. She is left with about $2 for other expenses such as clothing, school supplies and school uniforms for her children.

Sanjuana Orrdaz is the sole provider for her family of four children. She earns about $25 a week at the Ertl Company and uses the pay to support her children [from left] Gustavo, 9; a 3-month-old baby; Juan Antonia, 12; and Karina, 6.

She works because she must, even though it has driven her away from her husband. "My husband drank a lot. Besides that, he didn't work, and he didn't let me work because he was jealous," said Orrdaz. Money was scarce. "My oldest boy fainted several times in school because he didn't have enough to eat," she said.

So she left her husband and went back to work, she said, because her children, fourth-grader Juan Antonio, 12; second-grader Gustavo, 9; Karina, 6; and a 2- or 3-months-old baby girl that hadn't been named, didn't have enough to eat. The boys go to school, and a niece takes care of Karina and the baby while Orrdaz is at work.

"I couldn't bear to see my children suffer, so I left my husband and asked for my job back at Ertl," she said. "The first time my husband left me, he said he was going to change, that he would stop drinking. So we got back together, and that's when the baby was born." Now she and the children are on their own again. The children, bright and lively with big dark eyes and ready smiles, were excited as their mother arrived with visitors. She talked to them, cuddled the baby, then began the evening meal.

"I get home about 7:15 p.m. I clean house, wash dishes, prepare dinner and food for the next day," she said. This meal was just a few tortillas and a hot drink called "atole" made with flour, milk and water. Asked what she usually fixes for supper, she said, "Atole, sometimes with bread, sometimes with bean tacos."

Orrdaz said she can afford to buy a few eggs, potatoes, tomatoes, onions, flour and canned milk for the baby each week, "and every once in a while a little piece of meat and some fruit. I wash clothes and we bathe on Saturdays. I go to church when I have time. When I go to bed, I pray for myself and my children," she said.

Her bare, three-room dwelling, like most workers' homes in the border towns, has no running water. There's a privy in the front yard. The house, its battered panel walls dotted with religious pictures and family photographs, is sparsely furnished, with two beds and two flimsy chests in the bedroom-living area. There's an old black-and-white TV on one of the chests. The baby sleeps in a cardboard box on one of the beds. The kitchen is bare, with just a table, a glass water bottle and a one-element hot plate.

A third room, dark and empty, has a dirt floor and a ring of burnt wood and ashes where the family had built fires. There's also a porch, where Orrdaz washes her family's clothes on a concrete scrub board in a big metal tub.

She and other workers at Ertl feel lucky, she said, noting that many

Ertl workers were laid off last year after the toy company finished a big job for McDonald's Corporation and employment dropped to 85 from 225. She has no idea how the laid-off workers were chosen: "They just called people in and told them there was no more work, and they would have to let them go."

Asked what she would like her daughter to do when she's grown, Orrdaz said: "I don't want her to work in the maquilas. With God's help, she will have the studies so she can do something better. There are so many things that are better than what I am doing." Later, Bernal, the 24-year-old interpreter, said: "Sometimes I wonder how these people even survive. But I would say they [Orrdaz and her children] have rather good living conditions compared to others I have seen. At least they have the water delivered, and they don't have to pay rent.

"That's one of the things that help the owners of the maquilas. These people of the lower classes are just happy to have a place to live. They don't want trouble. They don't want the unions or syndicates, as they are called here. They just want their jobs."

Tijuana, Mexico— Sanjuana Orrdaz, 40, mixes "atole," a combination of rice flour, powdered milk, and water. She lives a meager existence on a hard scrabble hill on the outskirts of town. She makes $4.28 per day from Ertl de Mexico. Her son Gustavo, 9, is seated at the left.

12. Zenith

REYNOSA, MEXICO—Shuttle buses clog the streets, their pipes spewing fumes, their motley bodies revealing layers of colorful paint. Street vendors peddle fruit and other refreshments as young women— some wearing designer clothes, others in rural peasant garb—stream from the buses into the factories. Inside, the women punch time clocks, don smocks, and head for work stations on the vast, modern assembly floor.

Another day in Mexico has dawned for Zenith Electronics Corporation, the largest maquiladora employer here with 7,500 employees and one of the largest in Mexico with 18,700 workers scattered in five northern cities.

Pressed by competition from Far East electronics firms, Zenith started its Mexican quest for lower labor costs in the early 1970s with a small maquiladora, or export-oriented plant, 60 miles east of here in Matamoros. Today, the Matamoros plant, which makes remote-control devices, tuners, and electronic guns for picture tubes, employs close to 3,500 workers.

"About 1973 is when we started the move offshore. It was a case of trying to keep our head above water. When your cost of manufacturing exceeds your sales prices, you're in trouble," said Vince Kamler, Zenith's director of Mexican operations. The move followed an industry trend. "We followed RCA. They held off as long as they could, then moved to Mexico, and we followed," said Kamler.

Register Staff Writer Lou Ortiz assisted in reporting this story.

96

The decision turned out to be a critical one for the giant electronics manufacturer. The maquiladora program, with its low labor costs and special tariff breaks, "has allowed Zenith to remain competitive with companies in the Far East," said Kamler, adding that the move "was necessary for survival of the company."

Zenith's big shift to Mexico began in 1977 when the company opened a 100,000-square-foot plant in Reynosa for TV subassembly work. Later that year, Zenith announced that it planned a major manufacturing shift to Mexico and Taiwan, a move that cut more than 5,000 U.S. production jobs.

A U.S. victim of the decision was the company's plant in Sioux City, Iowa, with about 1,500 employees then. The plant, Sioux City's largest employer at the time, was shut down by July 1978. Some of its compo-

This is one of the giant assembly plants run by Zenith in Reynosa, Mexico. Zenith employs more than 7,500 workers in Reynosa and 18,700 in all of Mexico.

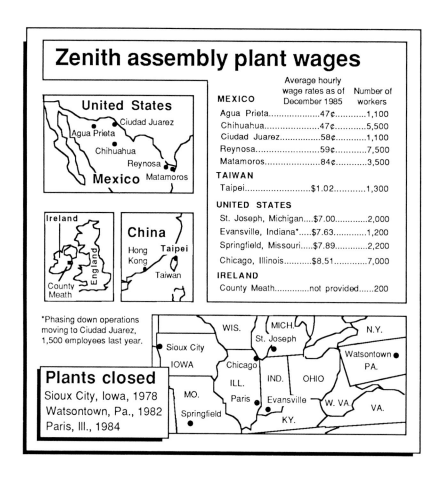

nent work was moved to Reynosa. Its stereo chassis work was eliminated when Zenith decided to buy ready-made stereo sets from the Orient.

Operations in Springfield, Missouri; Paris, Illinois; Watsontown, Pennsylvania, and the Chicago area also were cut back. The Paris and Watsontown plants eventually were closed, and Zenith began phasing out operations at its Evansville, Indiana, wood cabinet plant earlier this year. The Evansville plant's production is being shifted to a giant 629,000-square- foot plant in Ciudad Juarez, which eventually may employ 1,500 to 2,000 workers.

Operations in Reynosa, meanwhile, have grown steadily over the years, with production overflowing into four buildings with a total of 600,000 square feet of space. The complex, which makes circuit boards, microcircuits, and other components for final television assembly in Springfield, began its own assembly work last year when Springfield's 13-inch and low-priced 19-inch color TV assembly were shifted to Reynosa.

Kamler, recently promoted to vice president for consumer products, said the Reynosa complex can assemble 500,000 television sets a year, and will be able to assemble 1 million annually by the end of 1986. Zenith assembles about 2.5 million color sets annually, he said.

The massive Reynosa operation utilizes a unique blend of advanced technology and cheap Mexican labor to produce TV parts and components. While a few workers have acquired some technical knowledge, most technology is used to subdivide and simplify tasks, producing highly standardized, repetitious work that requires little technical knowledge. "We've got the largest automatic insertion area anywhere in the world," said Kamler, touring a giant room full of machines that automatically insert components on printed TV circuit boards. "It's a world-class facility."

The latest in robotics, automation, microchip technology and lasers are used here. Young women, paid about $4 a day, sit at stations up and down the assembly lines, positioning components, pressing switches, and monitoring the automatic insertion work. "Each operator is responsible for the quality of her machine," said Kamler. ". . . Our girls love to work. I'm amazed at what they do."

Kamler said the company is installing new Japanese-made insertion machines that will insert 320 components every 18 seconds and will almost triple the production of each machine. "Zenith has chosen us as a testing ground for robots because, in the test stage, if something goes

As nearly completed Zenith TV sets roll slowly by in a Reynosa, Mexico, plant, a worker tests the circuits of the sets.

wrong, we can bring in low-cost labor in place of the robots," said Kamler.

In another section of the manufacturing complex, Edwin McNeill, an Onawa, Iowa, native, directs Zenith's sophisticated microcircuit division, where 150 young women spend their days staring through microscopes, manipulating microchips, resistors and state-of-the-art relays.

A cartoon on McNeill's office wall depicts "the composite U.S. consumer," a grinning good ol' boy wearing a cowboy hat and sitting in a pickup truck. He has an AM/FM tape deck made in Mexico, a truck made in Japan, tires made in Germany, gasoline from Saudi Arabia, a shirt from Korea, a hat from Taiwan, and a license plate made in the United States. "I'm sold," says the caption.

Asked about the cartoon and his role as a manager in a U.S. operation in Mexico, McNeill said: "It bothers me, personally. All these manufacturing and production jobs are moving overseas. I buy only U.S. myself, but here I am, directing an off-shore operation. Right now, there's nothing that can be done about it, but something should be done."

Kamler predicted, however, that Zenith "will continue to shift production to Mexico," with employment possibly increasing another 3,000 to 4,000 in the next few years. And Ray Norton, a McAllen, Texas, advertising agency owner retained to act as a spokesman and publicist for Zenith's Mexican operations, said:

"Within three years, I predict almost all of Zenith will be in Mexico, with the exception of administration, research and development. Vince has a boss [in Springfield] who retires in a year and a half. I predict when he retires and Vince is promoted, he'll move that position down here."

Asked if workers in Springfield should be worried about losing their television assembly jobs, Kamler said, "Absolutely. . . . I would like to see the Springfield operation shut down and all the production moved here. I feel, long range, Zenith is going to be in trouble if it doesn't get its costs down. So why not move it down here where the costs are lower?"

Mexico is the best place in the world for Zenith to be making television sets, said Kamler. It is "a much better place to be than Taiwan. There's a shorter supply line and plenty of labor at comparable wage rates. Also, it's easier to get technical assistance here. Our managers can keep their families in the United States, and our operations help the economy" in southern Texas, he said.

Kamler said he would like to start buying picture tubes from a company in Monterrey, Mexico, instead of from Zenith's tube plant in

Illinois, a move that would increase the Mexican content of television sets assembled in Reynosa, and may allow him to sell television sets in Mexico. "I could sell another 100,000 sets in Mexico. That's a 5 percent increase in market. That's not bad," he said.

He also indicated that, besides trying to take Springfield's assembly work, he might push to have the company's plastic cabinet molding operation shifted from Springfield to Reynosa, too. Currently, tubes for smaller sets are shipped from Zenith's tube plant in Melrose Park, Illinois, to Springfield, where the tubes are placed in the plastic cabinets and shipped in their cartons to Reynosa for final assembly.

Kamler was asked what would happen if Zenith workers in Mexico successfully fought for higher wages: "If wages were to get too high in Mexico, Zenith and other companies would just move to other low-wage areas in the world. . . . What we're trying to do is get them to understand that their competition is the Far East, and even the Caribbean basin, where wages are even lower."

Asked if it bothers him to see manufacturing jobs leaving the United States, Kamler said: "It bothers me, and it bothers the daylights out of me that it's still continuing, but northern labor is pricing itself out of the market. The auto industry is moving out, too, and they're taking their vendors with them. . . . Everything I do, it's not to build a kingdom. I've got a few years left, and I want to finish my career at Zenith. We have to continue to move into Mexico because we don't see an end to the cost cutting by our competitors. It's either move to Mexico or cease doing business."

13. Sioux City Blues

SIOUX CITY, IOWA—It's been more than seven years since Zenith Electronics Corp. closed its doors here, cutting 1,500 jobs from the local economy. But six or eight loyal friends still meet each week to share lunch and memories of working for what was the city's largest employer. "It was rough when it closed. It was breaking up a family," said Hazel King, 66, sitting with her friends in a local cafe.

Shirley Menefee, 46, remembers her first day on the job. "I was thinking, 'I can't go to work in a factory—too rough, too tough,'" said Menefee, who now works in a K Mart pharmacy. "It wasn't like that at all. It was like a social club. I had 12 years there, a good work record because I didn't want to miss work. I loved it."

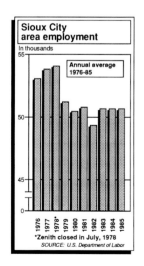

Sioux City area employment
In thousands
Annual average 1976-85
*Zenith closed in July, 1978
SOURCE: U.S. Department of Labor

Menefee has been with K Mart for 6½ years now: "I love it there, I really do, but the money isn't what I was making at Zenith." She started at $3.35 an hour and now makes $5.85, just a little more than the hourly rate she was making at Zenith more than seven years ago.

Rose McNaughton, 47, who cleans offices now, said she and her husband "gave up a cabin cruiser, a motor home, and two snowmobiles" after the plant closed. "I'm down to one car," she said. But it's not the luxuries she misses most: "They took more than a paycheck away from us. They took a way of life."

Richard Sturgeon, former business representative for the International Association of Machinists, the union that represented Zenith's workers here, said the women's sentiments and memories aren't that unusual, and with good reason. About 90 percent of the workers were

women, he said, and Zenith was one of the few places in town where they could earn decent wages, about $5 an hour at the time the plant closed.

"To this day, there are no jobs in Sioux City to replace the ones those women lost. These were proud women who had gone off welfare to work at Zenith, divorcees, single mothers and widows, or women who had left the home to help support the family," he said. And the women were loyal to Zenith, he added. "We had one lady, she was at the plant at 6 o'clock every day, even though work didn't start until seven. The plant was her life. It was that way with a lot of them," said Sturgeon.

The closing came as a shock, he said, because John Nevin, Zenith's chairman at the time, had just visited the plant and praised the operation. Nevin told the workers that "the Sioux City plant was one of the most productive in the Zenith chain. He said we had just about the best workers, the best attendance," Sturgeon recalled. "Then just a few months later . . . we're given the announcement that Zenith was cutting 5,000 jobs in the United States."

[From left] *Shirley Menefee, 46; Hazel King, 66; Betty Ege, 62; and Rose McNaughton, 47; were Zenith production line workers until the Sioux City plant behind them closed. The building now houses an auto parts manufacturing plant.*

Most people here agree that the closing hurt the community—at least in the beginning. The unemployment rate for the area jumped to 7.3 percent in 1979 from 5.9 percent the year before. Total employment declined to 51,200 from 54,100. Small business owners supplying parts and services to Zenith were hit. Automobile dealers, retailers and real estate businesses were hurt, too.

There is disagreement, however, about the long-term effects. Gary Hopp, district director for Job Service of Iowa here, pointed to the area's employment figures, which have been hovering between 50,000 and 51,000: "I would say no, the area hasn't recovered because those jobs were never totally replaced. Maybe some of those people are working now, but not at the wage they were before."

But many business leaders and local boosters disagree with Hopp's assessment. "The impact was substantial for three or four years . . . but I think now we have fully recovered from that closing," said Thom Rubel, acting president of the Siouxland Association of Business and Industry. He and others noted that Rochester Products, a fuel systems subsidiary of General Motors Corp., bought the Zenith plant in 1980. While the plant employs only 300 workers, having it occupied has provided a psychological boost, they say.

The city has enjoyed more than just psychological boosts, they add, noting that Sioux City is one of four Iowa cities that has had an increase in population since 1980. Retail sales are up, too, having increased 18 percent to $650 million in 1984 from $550 million in 1980. "At the same time, I think the state had a retail sales decline of 18 percent," Rubel noted.

Rubel and others said there are other signs of progress. United, America West and Republic Express airlines have joined Ozark and Eastern Air Midwest Express here, and Republic Express recently said it would move its maintenance and crew base to Sioux City from Aberdeen, S.D., which eventually will mean 200 new jobs.

Almost $90 million in construction was completed last year, is under way, or is scheduled to begin this year, said Gail Bernstein, director of research for the association. That includes new retail stores, new city buildings and new or remodeled shopping centers.

Also, a new telemarketing company, Long Lines Ltd., is gearing up just south of Sioux City. Long Lines is projecting eventual employment of 1,400 and a $25 million annual payroll. "I personally feel people have confidence in Sioux City and its future," said Bernstein.

14. Sweating in Springfield

SPRINGFIELD, MISSOURI – A giant poster in the Zenith factory here features a big American flag with workers' faces in place of stars. It reads: "MADE IN U.S.A., A Reputation Starring EVERYONE!"

But "U.S.A." is crossed out; "Mexico" has been penciled in. It's apparent what is on workers' minds. Zenith jobs have been moving from Springfield to Mexico for eight years, and they're wondering if the southbound shift ever will stop. Production employment here peaked in the early 1970s at about 4,200, then plunged to 1,100 in 1979 after Zenith moved its TV parts, chassis and subassembly production to Reynosa, Mexico.

Employment at the sprawling 1.7-million-square-foot plant, Springfield's largest industrial employer, increased to about 2,400 after Zenith agreed to shift some production here from Chicago. The union got the jobs by agreeing to lower differential pay for night workers.

Nevertheless, Zenith started shuffling jobs from Springfield to Mexico again last May, moving some of the factory's final assembly work to Reynosa, an ominous move for workers here because final assembly is the Springfield plant's bread and butter.

About 80 production workers lost their jobs when the company moved its 13-inch color TV production to Reynosa last year, and another 245 were cut earlier this year after Zenith decided to move some of Springfield's 19-inch TV production to Mexico and shut down the plant's second shift.

"We had 2,160 members working last spring. We're down to 1,741 now," said Bob Mingus, business manager of the International Brotherhood of Electrical Workers Local 1453. Workers here aren't talking of actions against the company, however. Instead, they've formed a "Buy American" committee and are lobbying for protective legislation for the U.S. television industry.

"Zenith is a cooperative company to work with," said Ray Edwards, an IBEW district vice president. "Zenith doesn't want to go to Mexico. There's no question about that. They'd like to keep their 'Made-in-the-U.S.A.' image right here in Springfield." He said, however, that he and union members here suspect that production will continue to shift to Mexico because of competitive pressures.

"Last year, they had the management and engineers here bidding for work against the Mexico operation, so of course it's beginning to shift. There's no way we can compete with the cheap labor in Mexico," he said. The average hourly wage in the Springfield plant was about $7.89 in December, compared with 59 cents at the company's Reynosa complex.

Zenith spokesman William Nail said executives have tried to keep workers informed of the company's plans, "and we have tried to make it clear that there are no intentions to move more assembly to Mexico." He added, "Our objective . . . is to preserve as many U.S. jobs as possible, but we have to cut costs to do so. The whole problem has been, to our sorrow, that our laws [related to dumping by foreign companies] have not been enforced.

"There's not a more efficient color TV plant in the world than our plant in Springfield, but you cannot compete with dumping," a tactic whereby foreign companies sell products for lower prices in the United States than they do in their own countries, he said. "They're giving away TV sets to gain market share."

William Schweikert, Zenith's operations manager in Springfield, said he and the other plant employees have a chance to keep the assembly of larger, more expensive television sets. "We know and understand the position of the company and the competitiveness of the marketplace. We do what we can, but it's an economic decision. If we can assemble sets for less than Zenith can in Mexico, then it will remain here," said Schweikert.

Zenith lost money in two of its last four fiscal years, including a $7.7 million loss in 1985, attributed to "severe price pressures in consumer electronics."

Meanwhile, workers here wait and worry in what one described as "a dread fear that it is going to go." Several expressed a feeling of helplessness during a group interview at the local union hall. "We ask,

Bob Kelly, 42, is among the dwindling number of production workers at the Zenith factory in Springfield, Missouri. "We deserve the truth," he says of fears that jobs like his could be lost to sites in Mexico.

'What can we do?' The answer is, we can't do enough to keep our jobs here," said Bill Raymond, 42.

"They want you to keep their production up," added James Johnson, 39. "They want you to move, to keep doing your best until they're ready to move, and then they move no matter what you've done. You can't compete with 50-cents-an-hour labor. I don't care what you do."

"After 19 years, we deserve the truth," said Bob Kelly, 42. "If they're going to Mexico, then tell us, and go. There's people who are worried sick."

Mingus acknowledged that formation of the "Americans for Americans" committee amounts to a last-ditch effort. "If they moved the 13-inch down there for survival, and it helps the company to survive to move the low-priced 19-inch TVs down there, they'd have to be patriotic as hell not to move more down there," he said. "I think, in time, you'll see a major warehouse here, at best."

Television assembly line workers leave the Zenith plant in Springfield, Missouri. Many of these workers share concerns that they could one day be asked to leave permanently, that Zenith could close this plant as it did another in Sioux City.

15. Struggling in Reynosa

REYNOSA, MEXICO—The Zenith plants are peaceful now. The red and black flags, fashioned from young women's slips, no longer fly as Mexico's standard strike symbol. The work aprons, splashed with demands for higher wages, no longer hang on fences.

Only memories of perhaps the largest strike ever against a U.S. company in Mexico remain among workers at Zenith's four plants in Reynosa—memories of firings, jailings, threats, and a few moments of triumph.

Many, however, inspired by soft-spoken Daniel Lopez, still are determined to press the fight for workers' rights. Zenith officials say the dispute is not their fault, that it is the result of internal union leadership struggles. But the current and former Zenith workers say they are fighting both the company and weak union leadership for better wages, a ban on forced overtime and other alleged workplace abuses.

Several attempts to reach top union officials in Reynosa were unsuccessful.

The problems began here in 1983 after the workers, mostly young women between 16 and 24, saw successive peso devaluations send wages plummeting from $10 a day down to $3.36. Lopez, in his teens at the time, was working as a "materials handler," keeping production lines stocked with supplies from the warehouse.

"The supervisors used to like me, and they would give me a lot of

---

Register Staff Writer Lou Ortiz assisted in the reporting for this story.

overtime," said Lopez, now 21. "But a lot of people couldn't work over-time because they had families to take care of. The company would force them to work and threatened them if they wouldn't. For about two months, during the summer of 1983, we were working 12-hour days, and only getting paid for 11 hours."

Lopez, a man with what some describe as "quiet charisma," said he and other workers got "fed up" and decided not to work one day in August: "About 75 of us stayed home. We wanted to teach the company and the union a lesson, and we wanted the injustices to end."

When the dissidents came to work the next day, company and union officials wanted to know who instigated the strike but no one would talk, said Lopez. Eventually, they gathered the workers and "apologized for not paying us the full 12 hours. They said we would start receiving the full pay for the following week."

The trouble didn't stop there. In October, Lopez and 11 other workers formed a dissident "Green slate" of union officer candidates and went to Mexico City to talk to Fidel Velazquez, the 85-year-old head of Mexico's dominant labor union, the Confederacion de Trabajadores de Mexico. Among other things, they wanted Velazquez's help in raising hourly pay to 60 cents from 42 cents. Velazquez wouldn't talk to the delegation, said Lopez.

Matters came to a head on November 5, after reports circulated that one of the union leaders had been kidnapped, beaten, and dumped near a lagoon. Lopez and his group met on a Sunday to discuss the "faked kidnapping, and we came to the conclusion that it was an attempt to destroy our movement."

The police were waiting for Lopez on Monday when he arrived at work. He was arrested as the instigator of the alleged kidnapping and was taken to jail. "They wanted me to sign a confession . . . but I kept telling them that I had nothing to do with it. The police kept taunting me, kept pressuring me all night," said Lopez. About 2 A.M., a police officer armed with a butcher knife told Lopez he would be turned over to soldiers who would beat a confession out of him. "When a jeep full of soldiers pulled up at the station, I thought I was a dead man," he said, but the soldiers left.

Lopez said he was never charged, and the police finally let him go about 9 A.M. after several hundred workers assembled in front of the station and started chanting, "We want Daniel."

His arrest led to a five-day strike by Zenith workers, which spread to nearly all maquiladoras in Reynosa. No one crossed the picket lines.

After the fourth day, Velazquez arrived and informed Lopez that he

[Opposite] *Daniel Lopez* [seated] *and Crispin Guajardo were among leaders of a workers' rebellion at the Zenith plant in Reynosa, Mexico, in 1983. Though largely unsuccessful then, they continue to agitate for more pay and other improvements.*

would declare the strike illegal "and force us back to work under threat of arrest." But he also agreed to schedule union elections for November 20, Lopez recalled. The Green slate won, with 80 percent of the vote, but the union wouldn't recognize the results. Instead, Velazquez scheduled another election in January 1984, "and we beat the Red slate again," said Lopez.

The results of that election were not recognized either, said Lopez, although some Green slate winners eventually were integrated into the union power structure.

A month after the election, however, Lopez and several other Green slate leaders were fired or forced to resign, Lopez said, and nearly 700 workers from Zenith and other plants were laid off and permanently replaced by new employees. In protest, Lopez and three other fired workers began a hunger strike in April in Reynosa's central plaza. Sipping fruit juice, they lay on cots surrounded by banners calling for the company to rehire the fired workers and to recognize the elected officers. After 13 days, police officers and Red Cross workers ended the protest, taking the group to a local hospital.

Scott Lind, a reporter for the McAllen *Monitor* in Texas who covered the hunger strikers' removal, also was arrested by Mexican police.

In a *Monitor* account of his overnight ordeal, Lind said that he was struck on the head and that interrogators "repeatedly applied electrical shocks to my testicles, my legs, my lips and sides" as they tried to find out whom Lind had talked to that day. He said he was told: "If you cooperate with us, you will be crossing the bridge within 30 minutes . . . But if you don't something very bad will happen to you. You'll be swimming face down in the river." Convinced his life was in danger, he told them what they wanted to hear, even signing a confession saying he and three others had kidnapped and raped Daniel Lopez.

He was released the next morning.

Several workers, including Lopez, said they, too, were told they would be "found floating in the river" if they didn't halt their dissident activities. But they say they have not given up. Many talked of problems, including allegations of sexual harassment inside the Zenith plants, but said they didn't want their names used. One, a 25-year-old woman, said: "There is a lot of talk of freedom of speech in Mexico, but it doesn't exist because whoever talks against the union or the company is fired."

A few agreed to speak openly. Maura Leti Leticia, 23, is an assembly line inspector, "but there's hardly a difference between what I earn and the people on the line. . . . I earn $3 to $4 a day, and we should

Reynosa, Mexico—
Daniel Lopez, a rebel
of sorts, who defied
the company, the
union, and the
police—and was
jailed by the latter.

be earning more when you consider that American workers doing the same jobs for Zenith are paid $8 an hour."

Paulina Hernandez Mendoza, 24, a Zenith assembly line worker, said she was pressured by the union to quit because of her support for

*Dina, Daniel Lopez'
daughter.*

the Green slate: "They would write me up, make up things, but I stuck it out."

Vince Kamler, Zenith's director of Mexican operations, said the Reynosa labor problems stem from infighting among union members and have little to do with Zenith. There's always a certain amount of labor unrest, he said: "For one thing, people aren't getting as much money as they think they should be getting."

But while wages in the U.S.-owned maquiladoras may seem low, he added, they're still higher than those in Mexican-owned plants. Employees can make "twice as much in maquilas, and the working conditions are much better. . . . Working conditions here are comparable or better than conditions in Zenith plants anywhere in the world," Kamler said.

In addition to the basic wage, he said, there are medical and other benefits and opportunities to advance to higher pay grades. The company also provides low-cost, subsidized meals in its cafeterias.

There were complaints of sexual harassment several years ago, Kamler said, but none in recent years. "It would be the sort of thing—'Have a date with me and I'll get you a job as an inspector'—that sort of thing. We've made it clear we don't condone that sort of thing. As a result, we don't see it anymore," he said.

". . . The workers here are very much on our side. . . . As long as they have a job and are treated fairly, they're happy. They don't take much interest in unions because they're so political." Kamler says there are always groups trying to seize power in the unions. "The leader of the local union receives his blessing from Mexico City. Once he has that, he does pretty much whatever he wants to do," he said. "When the union comes to us and tells us to terminate someone, we terminate them. . . . They have their struggles. Somebody always wins, and it's usually not the company." Zenith executives just try to keep the plant running smoothly, he said.

Lopez says he's keeping his eye on the Zenith situation, even though he no longer works there. "We have a new union boss in the area now, Jose Morales De La Cruz, and he hired me for a union job in January. I pick up the pesera (shuttle bus) drivers who transport the Zenith workers back and forth from their jobs," he said.

"The pesera is something we won through the movement. Before the movement, there was no transportation for the workers. Cruz is willing to listen and offers hope, [but] if things don't change, we'll get together and figure out a way of getting rid of him, too, and decide on other things to do to correct the injustices. . . . "

16. Hazards across the Border

TIJUANA, MEXICO – Some U.S. corporations are exporting health and safety hazards as well as jobs when they move operations to Mexico, according to Dr. Monica Jasis, one of a handful of academics who have studied health problems among Mexican workers in U.S.-owned plants.

However, the companies that operate the export-oriented factories known as maquiladoras disagree with Jasis, saying safety and health standards in their Mexican facilities are no different from those in the United States, even though Mexican laws aren't as stringent.

Jasis, a researcher with El Colegio de la Frontera Norte, says she found a high incidence of health problems among the young female workers she studied in Tijuana in 1982 and 1983, problems ranging from ill health linked to lead inhaled in soldering fumes, to eye problems caused by spending eight or more hours a day peering through microscopes while bonding fine wires to circuit boards.

"We worked in one plant, an electronics plant with 300 workers in 1983. It was a case study of 54 women. . . . Seven of the women I interviewed had had miscarriages, and all had been working with acetone during pregnancy," she said.

"We found heart and blood pressure problems related to stress, also the effects of hazardous substances which are prohibited in the United

---

Register Staff Writer Lou Ortiz assisted in the reporting for this story.

States—epoxy, resins, and TCE used to clean electronics parts and chips."

Of the 54 women, 85 percent had health problems that appeared to be linked to the work environment, and there was an occupational disability rate of 35.7 percent, Jasis said. Jasis wasn't surprised by her findings, she said, adding, "It is common to find the work with higher risks along the border. In Mexico, there are no prohibitions of specific substances. The regulations are very old and not very specific."

In Matamoros, Profesora Isabel Alonso, director of the School of Special Education, says she has been investigating a possible relationship between exposure to hazardous chemicals and worker health problems. She became interested when about 15 retarded children with birth

Matamoros, Mexico— A worker's hand dips a circuit board into a fuming open pool of molten solder. Left unventilated, the inhaled fumes can cause lung irritation. This picture was made in the Winegard plant. A hood above this woman ventilated the area.

defects, all near the same age, were enrolled at her school a few years ago. In checking the mothers' backgrounds, she found they had all worked at a maquiladora in the 1970s that used hazardous chemicals.

Alonso, a psychologist, says she has completed case histories of the mothers and the children, documenting psychological characteristics and the severity of the mental disorders of each child. Now, she said, she is seeking financing to conduct a genetic study of the women and their children to see if there is scientific evidence of a mutagenic effect caused by chemicals.

"I haven't and won't give up until they're done. It's important to my people, their children, and present and future maquiladora workers," she said.

In Ciudad Juarez, there have been allegations that trichloroethylene (TCE), a carcinogenic chemical used by some U.S. electronics firms, has contaminated drinking water, according to Guillermina Valdes-Villalva, director of El Colegio de la Frontera Norte there. Also, newspapers there have charged that GTE Corporation has been moving its more hazardous electronics operations from New Mexico to Juarez.

GTE is the object of 75 lawsuits bearing charges of harming the health of former workers at a plant in Albuquerque, New Mexico, but company officials have denied that GTE has hazardous operations in either the U.S. or Mexico. They say corporate policy is to decline comment on pending lawsuits, but they believe the lawsuits are "without merit."

Valdes-Villalva said the Juarez press has sensationalized the GTE story, but part of the problem rests with the Mexican government. "The mere fact that Mexico has not placed limits on chemicals in the workplace is bound to have an effect. It's easier to operate here," she said.

Still, officials of companies with Mexican facilities say they don't use the lack of regulations as an excuse to operate substandard operations. Rather, they say, they maintain strict safety standards on both sides of the border. "We try to live up to as many OSHA (Occupational Safety and Health Administration) standards here as we would in the United States," said Vince Kamler, Zenith's director of Mexican operations. "We don't have to do that, but we try to live up to them."

Michael Wales, manager of Winegard Company's Mexican subsidiary in Matamoros, said safety standards there are just as strict as they are in the Burlington company's Iowa plants. Nevertheless Jasis and others on the Mexican side of the border say U.S. corporations have made it clear to the Mexican government that they do not want to be bothered with health and safety inspections at their plants. Jasis says she had to halt her studies because of growing opposition among maquiladora owners.

"The government's position is to provide convenience for the companies that locate here because they provide jobs, so they don't ask many questions," said Jasis, whose studies are funded by the government. "When we started to speak about our results, there was a lot of reaction. We wanted to continue with a census of workers' health, but it was not allowed" by the government, she said.

Maria Patricia Fernandez-Kelly, a researcher with the Center for U.S.-Mexican Studies at the University of California at San Diego, also believes maquiladora health problems are being downplayed. In February 1980, 35 workers employed by a subsidiary of Sylvania had to be rushed to a hospital in Ciudad Juarez, she said in a report about health and safety in maquiladoras. "Early reports indicated that a malfunctioning cooking vat containing trichloroethylene had produced hydrolyzed hydrochloric fumes which spread through the shop causing widespread nausea, vomiting, and loss of consciousness," she wrote.

"At first the local dailies confirmed the connection between the breakdown of the cooking equipment and the symptoms experienced by the workers. . . . However, only 24 hours later, the official joint report from the plant manager and the head of the Social Security Clinic . . . differed greatly. . . . Unanimously, the two now agreed that the incident had been a 'hysterical reaction to an imaginary ailment.' "

There is little visible effort under way to change health and safety standards in the maquiladoras. Jasis said she hasn't urged the government to begin regulating health and safety in the maquiladoras because her role is to conduct research and provide information. "There is no organization that has taken a stand on behalf of the maquiladoras and the problems they're having in regard to illnesses, injuries, or other hazards," she said.

17. Winners and Losers

Enrique Esparza sets up maquiladoras for a fee.

NATIONAL CITY, CALIFORNIA—Enrique Esparza, a smooth-talking entrepreneur, has watched his business grow by leaps and bounds, fueled by the demand for low-wage labor. For a fee, he'll provide everything a U.S. company needs to open a Mexican assembly plant, or maquiladora. The client provides an operations manager; Esparza finds the building, the equipment, even a Mexican personnel manager to hire the workers.

"It used to be mainly electronics, but now it's becoming more diverse. We have clients who manufacture eyeglass frames, waterbeds, wooden furniture, disposable medical products, and sprinkler systems," said Esparza, president of Assemble in Mexico Inc.

The company supervised operations involving 600 workers in 1984, grew to operations with 1,200 employees by the end of 1985, and Esparza expects it to double again this year. The reason is simple, he said: Workers in the maquiladoras collect just $4 to $7 per day, performing tasks once done by thousands of U.S. workers who have lost their jobs. "If we're going to stay competitive with the rest of the world, we'd better learn to use what is available in the world. You may end up buying parts in the Far East, assembling them in Mexico and selling the finished product in the United States," he said.

Mexican officials and U.S. executives say the explosion of U.S.-

Register Staff Writer Lou Ortiz assisted in the reporting for this story.

owned export plants has, on balance, been good for both countries, creating a "win-win" situation. Mexico has won a much-needed boost for its teetering economy; the plants now employ 260,000 workers. "Mexico has to produce 800,000 to 900,000 jobs a year just to absorb people entering the work force, and the country can't do it. The maquila program has helped to alleviate that problem," said Bert Diamondstein, with the El Paso (Texas) Industrial Development Corp.

Meanwhile, some American companies have won a competitive advantage in the face of growing international pressures. "We have a major share of our manufacturing in Mexico, and it's primarily to try to stay alive," said Vince Kamler, Zenith Electronics Corp's operations manager in Mexico. And if U.S. companies are stronger because of the maquiladoras, "it should mean more jobs in Mexico and the United States," said Esparza.

Zenith, which shuttered a large plant in Sioux City, Iowa, in 1978, now employs 18,700 people in Mexico. Company officials say that if it weren't for those workers, 12,000 Zenith jobs in the U.S. would be in jeopardy because the company wouldn't be able to remain competitive with Far East firms using "dumping" tactics.

Officials of three Iowa-based companies with Mexican operations echo the Zenith philosophy. Jay Bristol, a vice president with Clinton's Nielsen Clearing House, says his company probably would be out of business if it weren't for its Mexican coupon-sorting operations because coupon handling costs would be prohibitive. As it is, the business has grown and Nielsen still has 600 office workers in Clinton. Officials at Dyersville-based Ertl say that company's Mexican plant has allowed Ertl to expand into lower-priced products and to compete more effectively with other toy firms, making 800 jobs in Iowa more secure. And officials at Burlington-based Winegard Company say the products the firm makes in Mexico are products it would have to buy from Far Eastern sources because of world competition. The Mexican plant has made the company stronger and has helped preserve 220 production jobs in Iowa, they say.

Iowa and other U.S. companies aren't the only ones satisfied with the results. Up and down the border, U.S. industrial development officials brush aside problems such as overtaxed highways and other city services, saying they see nothing but benefits from the maquiladora program.

Besides creation of jobs—on both sides of the border—they say Mexican workers typically spend 40 percent or more of their pay buying goods from U.S. retailers. "It has been a great assistance to our eco-

Growth of Maquiladoras.

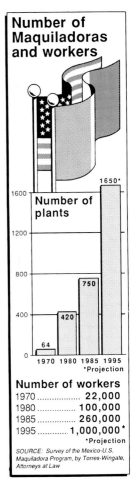

Number of Maquiladoras and workers

Number of plants

1600

1200

800

1650*

400

750

420

64

0

1970 1980 1985 1995
*Projection

Number of workers

1970	22,000
1980	100,000
1985	260,000
1995	1,000,000*

*Projection

SOURCE: Survey of the Mexico-U.S. Maquiladora Program, by Torres-Wingate, Attorneys at Law

nomic development, even though many of the jobs are across the border," says James Ebersole, industrial development manager for the Brownsville Chamber of Commerce. "The key people who run the plants live in Brownsville. We have more than 40 maquilas in Matamoros and 300 key people living in Brownsville."

People living or working on the U.S. side, along with retail sales to maquiladora workers, pump an estimated $2.6 million a month into the Brownsville economy, he said. Farther west, officials say 900 El Paso residents work as managers in the 180 Ciudad Juarez maquiladoras, which pump an estimated $300 million a year into El Paso's economy. Diamondstein, with the El Paso development group, said that in addition to more jobs, the maquiladoras are helping with a "transfer of technology and industrial skills" as northern Mexico moves rapidly from an agrarian-based economy and society to an industrial-based society.

Diamondstein acknowledged, however, that there are individual losers in the United States. "What do you tell the 50-year-old tool and die maker in the Midwest who's lost his job after working 30 years? There's probably not anything you can tell that man . . . but either you survive in today's competitive environment or you go under," he said.

Zenith executives say the migration of U.S. jobs to Mexico could have been prevented if the U.S. government had dealt with unfair trade practices by companies in the Far East. Instead, color TV imports continue to grow, increasing to 6.8 million sets in 1984 from 3 million in 1982. Zenith has had an antitrust and antidumping suit against the Japanese television industry in the federal court system since 1974, but the company has been unable to get the case to trial because of legal delay tactics, company officials say.

The firm contends that Japanese companies have dumped TV sets on the U.S. market at artificially low prices while maintaining substantially higher prices in Japan with the intent of monopolizing the business and destroying U.S. manufacturers. "We're not the only industry affected. Textiles, shoes, and others are suffering, too," said William Schweikert, Zenith's operations manager in Springfield, Missouri. "The dumping countries, they're just exporting their unemployment." Schweikert says Zenith executives are not advocating "unfair protectionism, just protection from unfair tactics by other countries." If the government doesn't help, "we will have two alternatives: go broke or go somewhere where we can do business profitably," he warned.

However, many officials say protective legislation is not the answer. It would only lead to higher prices for consumers and retaliatory measures by other countries. "That's not the way to solve the problem.

[Opposite] Dina Isabelle Lopez, 2, will grow up into a world of work in the maquiladora system. Her father, activist and rebel Daniel Lopez, would like her to have hopes of higher pay, safer working conditions, and better union representation.

The solution is a true free market," said Gene Dubrosky, a Winegard vice president. "What we can do here to stem the tide of imports is to improve our productivity, the way we do that is to be as good as *they* are."

Paul Volcker, chairman of the Federal Reserve Board, told the House Budget Committee recently that protectionist legislation could trigger "recession on a worldwide basis" when coupled with recent declines in oil prices and the dollar.

In Mexico, meanwhile, the debate centers on how well the maquiladora program has dealt with the country's poverty and economic problems. Experts generally agree that it hasn't made a significant dent in Mexico's unemployment. Instead of providing jobs for out-of-work Mexicans, the maquilas have lured a new group into the work force: young women in their teens and 20s. Wages are so low, they add, that most maquiladora workers remain in poverty.

The impact of maquiladoras in terms of broadening Mexico's industrial base and transferring technology has been limited, too, they say. "In the majority of cases, workers are trained to perform limited operations. . . . As most technical, professional, and managerial positions in the maquilas are held by personnel from parent companies, the potential for more extensive training of the typical Mexican worker is limited," according to a report written by Edward George and Robert Tollen, professors at the University of Texas at El Paso.

Maria Patricia Fernandez-Kelly, a maquiladora expert with the Center for U.S.-Mexican Studies at the University of California at San Diego, says advanced industrial nations such as the United States "retain control over research and development, technological expertise, decisions affecting production, and the direction of financial outflows," thus limiting any effective transfer of technology.

There are advantages for Mexico, however. George and Tollen say the maquiladoras are "producing good dividends to the Mexican government in foreign exchange." The foreign-owned export plants brought in about $1.4 billion last year, second only to the estimated $14.6 billion brought in by Mexico's petroleum industry.

Even in this area, however, some say the benefits have been exaggerated and are outweighed by social and other costs related to the rapid development of maquiladoras. "The maquiladora industry is a double-edged sword for the Mexican economy. It supplies short-term employment with very few long-term benefits, and many of the dollars earned here are spent in the United States because the products people want to buy are most available in the United States," said Rosalva Gal-

lardo, branch director of El Colegio de la Frontera Norte in Nogales, Mexico.

Fernandez-Kelly says she has studied maquiladoras from the "participant" and "case study" points of view because the tendency is to discuss them using broad terms. Her approach, she says, "shows workers as more than the 'cheap labor' they appear to be, when viewed from a global 'demands of capital' viewpoint." In one case study, she wrote: "After four years of tedious labor at the plant, Kika admits that she is exhausted. More discouraging than monotony is the realization that promotions are hard to come by and wages are forever shrinking. . . .

"To promoters of the maquiladora program in Mexico, export-directed industrialization is a success. But Kika lives in a bind that exposes the meaning of underdevelopment and dependency."

Fernandez-Kelly and other scholars don't advocate elimination of the maquiladora program. That would be unrealistic, they say. "Things you would normally be critical of, in a national emergency you have to live with them," said Guillermina Valdez-Villalva, director of El Colegio de la Frontera Norte in Ciudad Juarez. "I think that in the crisis Mexico finds itself in, we have to have very large numbers of people employed even to exist. So Mexico has had to adopt a strategy for survival."

What she and others would like to see is improved wages, working conditions, and job stability.

Ed Krueger, an American Friends Service Committee employee who has been working with maquiladora workers in Reynosa and Matamoros since 1979, says, "I don't think we're going to stop the maquiladora system. It's such a tidal wave, you have to be realistic. But I think Mexico is selling itself short. . . . The maquilas could pay a much better wage, and it would bring more dollars into Mexico.

"It costs one company here one-fourth of a cent in labor per pair of shoes. What difference would it make to raise that to half a cent and pay the workers double what they make? Sometimes they carry this exploitation to the point where it is ludicrous," said Krueger. "Make it more humane. Make it something we don't have to be ashamed of."

EPILOGUE

I THOUGHT it appropriate to conclude this book with an African parable related by Miriam Were to attendees at the World Food Conference in Des Moines in 1988. Were, a Kenyan, was a United Nations official working in Ethiopia at the time.

The parable is about a man with two huts. The man lived in one hut, his wife and children lived in the other. As the nights grew colder, the man felt a chill, so each night he took grass from the roof of his family's hut and put it on his own to keep out the cold. His friends asked him, "Why are you doing this?" He replied, "Because I need to keep warm." He continued, ignoring his friends and the chills of his family, until one morning he awoke to find his wife and children had died from the cold.

And so it is in the world today, said Were. Many cling to their comforts while others die.

That was the end of the parable, but Were went on to say that the issue of world hunger is "an issue of who is going to pay for the changes that must be made. Someone has to give. . . . The option is, you get a little cold or other people die. Those are the choices you make."